American Psychiatric Association
Symposium of the Hawaiian Divisional Meeting, 1958

SCHIZOPHRENIA

An Integrated Approach

Edited by

ALFRED AUERBACK, M.D.

ASSISTANT CLINICAL PROFESSOR OF PSYCHIATRY
UNIVERSITY OF CALIFORNIA SCHOOL OF MEDICINE, SAN FRANCISCO
SPEAKER, ASSEMBLY OF DISTRICT BRANCHES
AMERICAN PSYCHIATRIC ASSOCIATION

THE RONALD PRESS COMPANY · NEW YORK

List of Contributors

GREGORY BATESON, M. A., Ethnologist, Veterans Administration Hospital, Palo Alto, California, and Visiting Professor, Department of Anthropology, Stanford University.

RAY L. BIRDWHISTELL, Ph.D., Associate Professor, Department of Anthropology, and Coordinator, Institute for Research in Human Communication, University of Buffalo.

MURRAY BOWEN, M.D., Chief, Family Study Section, Clinical Investigations, National Institute of Mental Health, Bethesda, Maryland.

KARL M. BOWMAN, M.D., Professor of Psychiatry, Emeritus, the Langley Porter Neuropsychiatric Institute, University of California School of Medicine, San Francisco.

C. H. HARDIN BRANCH, M.D., Professor and Head, Department of Psychiatry, College of Medicine, University of Utah.

HENRY W. BROSIN, M.D., Professor and Chairman, Department of Psychiatry, University of Pittsburgh School of Medicine, and Director, Western Psychiatric Institute and Clinic, Pittsburgh.

JOY W. ELY, M.D., Teaching Assistant, Department of Psychiatry, College of Medicine, University of Utah.

ROBERT G. HEATH, M.D., Professor and Chairman, Department of Psychiatry and Neurology, Tulane University School of Medicine.

ROBERT A. KIMMICH, M.D., Chief, Professional Education, Stockton State Hospital, Stockton, California; formerly, Medical Director, Territorial Hospital, Kaneohe, Hawaii.

LAWRENCE C. KOLB, M.D., Professor and Chairman, Department of Psychiatry, Columbia University, College of Physicians and Surgeons, and Director, New York State Psychiatric Institute.

LESTER H. MARGOLIS, M.D., Assistant Clinical Professor, Department of Psychiatry, University of California School of Medicine, San Francisco.

JULES H. MASSERMAN, M.D., Professor of Neurology and Psychiatry, The Medical School, Northwestern University.

MILTON ROSE, M.D., Clinical Instructor in Psychiatry, University of California School of Medicine, San Francisco.

JURGEN RUESCH, M.D., Professor, Department of Psychiatry, University of California School of Medicine, and the Langley Porter Neuropsychiatric Institute, San Francisco.

FREDERIC G. WORDEN, M.D., Associate Research Psychiatrist and Associate Professor of Psychiatry, University of California School of Medicine, Los Angeles, and the Veterans Administration Hospital, Long Beach, California.

Preface

It is a paradox of modern psychiatry that the illness most commonly found in our mental hospitals is one about which there is still very little known. Until recently schizophrenia remained cloaked in the same mystery that has surrounded it since antiquity. However, in the past few years, stimulated in some degree by the advent of psychopharmacology, biochemical, neurophysiological, and brain metabolic studies have begun to offer some promising leads. Concurrently, psychiatrists have joined forces with sociologists, anthropologists, and ethnologists in the fields of communication and intra-family relationships. Most of this work in the field of schizophrenia is relatively unknown to the practicing psychiatrist.

In May, 1958, the Hawaiian Divisional meeting of the American Psychiatric Association was devoted to a symposium on schizophrenia where leading psychiatrists, anthropologists, ethnologists, and sociologists reviewed our present knowledge of this disorder. Amid a lush verdant setting several hundred psychiatrists met to discuss this problem and to exchange ideas.

The reader of this book will note that there are now many paths to travel in seeking the answers to schizophrenia, that no group or discipline alone will provide the solution. Only an integrated multidisciplinary approach will lead us to effective methods of treatment. This book reviews the progress that has been made in the last few years in the treatment of schizophrenia. The next ten or twenty years will surely produce even greater enlightenment. At that time we will be able to assess just how close we were to solution in 1958.

The editor wishes to thank the contributors for their wholehearted cooperation in preparing this book. Special thanks go to Dr. Norman Q. Brill of the University of California Medical School at Los Angeles who selected the topics and speakers for the symposium.

The royalties from the sale of this book will be given to the American Psychiatric Association.

ALFRED AUERBACK, M.D.

San Francisco, California

Contents

SCHIZOPHRENIA

An Integrated Approach

1

What Is Schizophrenia?

KARL M. BOWMAN [1] AND MILTON ROSE [2]

To know schizophrenia is to know psychiatry. Does this sound too pat or extravagant? I think not. Consider the frequency with which the term arises in the day-to-day differential diagnosis of mental disease. What discussion of psychopathology is complete without reference to it? What therapist, balked by nature or by his own inadequacy, does not at times make use of it to explain away therapeutic failure?

The term has become, since its introduction by Eugen Bleuler in 1911, so commonplace that one may safely say it has proved its utility as a means of conveying a clinical picture every psychiatrist can recognize. A moment's thought will make it apparent that schizophrenia is in practice so clearly understood, at least descriptively, that it stands out more distinctly as a clinical entity than almost any of the other so-called functional disorders of the mind.

Why, then, has the program committee of this association suggested that the first paper in this three-day symposium on schizophrenia be entitled "What is schizophrenia?" Would a surgical society initiate a three-day symposium on

[1] Professor of Psychiatry, Emeritus, University of California School of Medicine, San Francisco.
[2] Clinical Instructor in Psychiatry, Department of Psychiatry, University of California School of Medicine, San Francisco.

cancer of the breast with a paper called "What is cancer?"
Would a group of internists start off a series on bronchial
asthma with an address called "What is asthma?" The answer, of course, is a decided "yes." Such questions are highly
relevant to the discussion and understanding of all kinds of
medical and scientific subject matter.

What, actually, does the question mean, and why is it
properly raised at a meeting such as this? Why, indeed, does
the same question arise in almost any discussion of schizophrenia, from the casual conversation of medical colleagues
talking shop to the serious deliberations of a national gather-
ing of psychiatrists?

Two things at once come to mind. The first is the practical necessity of dealing with individual cases. We certainly
want to be able to recognize a case of schizophrenia when
we see it, and in psychiatric practice we inevitably run into
atypical cases which lie on the borderline of the classical
diagnostic picture summarized by the diagnostic term.
Diagnostic terms are, of course, generalizations which describe a cross-section picture of symptom complexes occurring together and running a more or less typical course.
Clearly, there will always be cases which do not conform to
the cross-section picture, and the question of their inclusion
or exclusion from the class will arise. The greater the knowledge available, particularly precise knowledge in terms of
anatomy and physiology, the better we can understand the
relations of the symptoms to each other and to the underlying disease process, and the less trouble we shall have in
making decisions about individual cases. Unfortunately, the
limits of application of most diagnostic terms in psychiatry
are relatively vague and the problem of borderline cases
is a frequent one.

Second, and more fundamental, in asking "What is schizophrenia?" we raise the question of the nature of the disease,
that is, its cause or causes as well as its manifestations,

course, and outcome. We ask for an explanation of why and how the disease occurs and what its relationship is to other disorders and to normal mental functioning. In other words, we ask for a scientific theory which will account for the phenomena we observe, a theory establishing the general laws which govern mental and emotional function and dysfunction.

These two meanings of the question "What is schizophrenia?" are equally important to psychiatrists. Unfortunately, they are not equally easy to answer.

A fairly exact answer can be given to the first question—the practical one of diagnosis or classification—and any one of you could give an answer which would be understood and accepted as in accord with the facts of clinical experience by most of our colleagues. The second question—the theoretical one—is more difficult, and although some of you might venture to attempt the sort of "explanation" demanded by the question, there is no assurance that your explanation would be understood or accepted by even a small number of our colleagues.

There have been explanations of this sort current at all times, in the past and in the present, and always there is a great deal of controversy as to the validity of the theories proposed. It is easy to see that final decisions cannot be reached about such theories until sufficient generally established knowledge has been accumulated to permit the scientific testing of the theories and their validation or refutation.

At present, the fund of such cumulative knowledge is sadly limited. It is thus important for us to realize that we are able to answer the question "What is schizophrenia?" in one way, at least. That is, we can diagnose cases of schizophrenia—even though on a purely descriptive basis—with a reasonably satisfactory amount of agreement for clinical and statistical purposes. Classification of this sort provides for the ordering of "public" observations and the possibility of

communication for practical purposes at a time when agreement and general understanding cannot be reached on the
basis of theoretical explanations. In spite of the limitations
on our theoretical knowledge, then, we do have adequate
diagnostic information and classificatory techniques to deal
with schizophrenia in clinical practice.

Diagnosis vs. Theory

Of the two basic meanings of the question forming the
title of this paper, that is, (1) the classification and clinical
diagnosis of cases, and (2) the nature of the disease process,
the first is a question of definition and the second a question
of theory. The two are often confused and are approached
in various ways without differentiating between them. Diagnosis is a basic scientific classificatory technique. Diagnostic
categories do not exist in nature, but are established for
scientific, administrative, therapeutic, and other purposes.
We separate out phenomena we observe to have certain
things in common which justify our grouping them together
in one class.

The definition of a diagnostic term will, like all good
definitions, specify the necessary and sufficient conditions
for class membership, will be clear and unambiguous, and
will provide for reliable and consistent classification. It will
be as inclusive as is consistent with clarity and precision in
application, will permit prediction, and, if possible, will indicate therapy. This latter is usually possible only if the diagnosis can be based on knowledge of etiology or if a correlation is established between the diagnostic picture and some
empirically developed therapy.

A diagnostic category is best based on scientifically
proved relationships between symptoms, course, outcome,
etc. But, depending upon the amount of such scientific
information available, the conditions prescribed for the inclu-

sion of individual cases within the category can vary from purely descriptive to precisely etiological or any combination of available classifying data.

Theories and inferences about the origin and meaning of symptoms and the disease process have no place in the actual definition of a diagnostic term, though they will often determine the kind of diagnostic criteria set up. If a theory is, in fact, scientifically established, it will certainly make possible the setting up of a definition which is a precise and clinically applicable statement of the conditions known to be essential for the appearance of the specific disease.

A definition is arbitrary and must only fulfill the logical and practical conditions already mentioned. A theory, on the other hand, attempts to explain the occurrence of certain phenomena and their relationship to each other. A theory is thus subject to scientific evaluation and must be rejected if if is found *not* to explain what it purports to explain. It must be couched in such terms as to permit testing and acceptance or rejection on the basis of repeated experience. Scientific objectivity stems, not from the actual or attempted objectivity of individual scientists, but from the cooperation of many scientists who are ready to criticize and be criticized, to subject their theories and hypotheses to the test of public experience—that is, to the repeated observations and experiments of others.

A great many explanations of what goes on in schizophrenia have been proposed and attempts made to account for the clinical data by relating them to one theoretical framework or another. There are explanations which are largely psychodynamic, cultural or sociological, psychosomatic, biological (including hereditary) and biochemical. When the question "What is schizophrenia?" is discussed with respect to which of these explanations or what combination of them is the answer to the question, it appears that the problem is extremely complicated and that a vast amount of data must be taken into account in obtaining the correct answer.

We can, however, avoid being overwhelmed by trying to reconcile all this conflicting and confusing material at our disposal from the natural and social sciences usually considered applicable to the field of psychiatry. To do so, we must keep in mind that we are dealing with two questions and two kinds of data. First, we have the "public" clinical data and a certain amount of proved scientific information. Second, there is a large amount of data which is only inferentially applicable to the question "What is schizophrenia?" That is not to say that these data are irrelevant or that the inferences drawn from them are incorrect. But their relevance can be considered only in the light of the theories proposed to establish such relevance. Examples of the sort of data referred to here are inferences as to the relationship of broken homes, slums, etc., to the development of schizophrenia, the relationship of the "rejecting mother" to schizophrenia, or the relationship of disturbances in brain metabolism to schizophrenia. Such inferences are plainly a different type of data from clinical facts, such as the observed relationship of the occurrence of flattening of affect and fragmentation to schizophrenia. Inferences of the sort mentioned above have generally not been established as necessary and sufficient conditions for the appearance of schizophrenia, either because they have not been proved to be necessary or sufficient or because they are not subject to or are difficult to subject to investigation and verification through the application of scientific method.

Historical Review

Bleuler's [3] *schizophrenia* is now almost a half century old. The term and the concept it represents were introduced to

---

[3] Eugen Bleuler (1857–1930), Swiss psychiatrist, renamed the syndrome of dementia praecox *schizophrenia* and made the term more inclusive.

replace the term *dementia praecox,* coined originally in 1860 by Benedict Morel,[4] who used it in a limited and special way. Dementia praecox gained wide usage and fame when Emil Kraepelin,[5] the grand master of psychopathological classification, reintroduced it and gave it a new meaning in 1896, fifteen years before Bleuler suggested the word *schizophrenia* as a more useful substitute.

The definition of the term *schizophrenia* as in use today is expressed almost entirely with reference to public and purely descriptive data about symptoms, their manifestation, course, and the outcome of the disorder. This definition is based on essentially the same data as those used by Bleuler in setting up the original definition. It seems safe to say that the many theories and speculations which have been offered about the nature of the disorder, its etiology, its relationship to other disorders, and to normal mental and emotional functioning have added little to our cumulative, generally accepted knowledge about schizophrenia. Any such contributions would surely be reflected in a changed definition of the term, and in practice we still rely on clinical observation of symptoms and course to establish the diagnosis. And in practice the term is useful because psychiatrists are able to recognize the essential symptoms and by applying the term *schizophrenia* to communicate to others their judgment about the presence of schizophrenia in a given case.

Since Kraepelin and Bleuler were the originators of the modern nosology of schizophrenia, it might be useful to review very briefly their work and its influence on modern psychiatry, for this influence today is much more important than has usually been realized.

[4] Benedict A. Morel (1809–1873), French psychiatrist and physiologist, known for his work on degeneration among the mentally ill and his view that degeneration was the result of hereditary weakness. He introduced the term *dementia praecox.*

[5] Emil Kraepelin (1856–1926), German psychiatrist, further differentiated and defined mental disorders, i.e., manic-depressive insanity and dementia praecox.

Bleuler proposed the term *schizophrenia* in a spirit of modesty and with emphasis on the fact that Kraepelin's concept of dementia praecox was of the first order of importance to psychiatric nosology and to thought about mental disease in general. Bleuler expressed the opinion that Kraepelin's observations and thinking brought order out of chaos in psychiatric nosology by unifying under the term *dementia praecox* a group of mental symptoms which had appeared to have little relationship to one another and which had created no end of confusion in thinking about mental disorders. Only a study of psychiatric writing before Kraepelin can give us today a clear picture of the confusion which then existed with regard to classification. We heartily recommend such a study to those who at times feel overwhelmed by the complexities of twentieth-century psychiatric practice.

Kraepelin's devotion to the task of clarifying nosology has led to a traditional view of him as a man more interested in the disease than in the patient. He was a great innovator in nosology. He saw a relationship between several psychiatric syndromes—among hebephrenia, paranoia, and catatonia—combined them into one disorder, and clearly distinguished them from manic-depressive disease. Kraepelin described this new classification, dementia praecox, as a functional disease without known physical cause and without consistently demonstrable anatomical basis, though he believed it was probably endocrinal in origin. At first he listed the characteristics of the disease as: (1) a beginning early in life, usually about the time of adolescence, and (2) a course that was almost always downhill, a phenomenon to which he applied the now familiar term *deterioration*. Later, after 1899, he also included in the category cases which could be resolved or arrested for long periods of time. His later definition also indicated that the disorder could first show itself in a florid form in the middle or later years of life. This fact, namely Kraepelin's inclusion under dementia praecox of cases

which were not deteriorating and which began after adolescence, has not been fully appreciated.

Bleuler had spent some time with Sigmund Freud around
the turn of the century and was influenced by Freud's depth
psychology and the concept of the unconscious. Employing
this concept and the idea of the importance of early experience in the development of the personality, Bleuler sought
to explain many of the phenomena of schizophrenia in psychological terms. It was largely because of this that he came
to be known for his interest in the patient as well as in the
disease. But he had accepted the essentials of Kraepelin's
system of classification, and his improvements upon it were
mostly by condensation and clarification and by giving it a
new name. The new name was suggested in order to get
away from the stress on dementia and deterioration and the
notion that the disease always began early in life.

Bleuler's revision of the basic Kraepelinian description of
schizophrenia established two sets of symptoms: primary, or
Grundsymptoma, and secondary. Primary symptoms were
disturbances of thought (chiefly, fragmentation), disturbances of affect (often, though not always, in the form of
flattening of affect), and ambivalence, a term which Bleuler
invented. Secondary symptoms included those which frequently appeared in other mental disorders, for example,
delusions, hallucinations, ideas of depersonalization, etc.
Simple schizophrenia, one of Bleuler's four subgroups, consisted of *Grundsymptoma* only.

Clinical Picture

Whatever controversies may exist as to theory about
schizophrenia, there is agreement as to the clinical picture.
We look for the Bleulerian primary and secondary symptoms, and we can still observe that the disease in a high
proportion of cases is chronic and recurrent even though
deterioration will not be apparent in the majority of cases.

In most instances, the onset or "break" occurs early in life. Even in those atypical cases which cause such difficulty, the cases are recognized as possible atypical cases of a known disease pattern. Certainly at this stage in our knowledge, we could not hope to establish a diagnostic category that would be 100 per cent applicable, with no possibility of borderline cases.

Borderline cases are, after all, common, indeed inevitable, in all fields of medicine. This is because some condition (sign or symptom) considered necessary or sufficient for clinching a diagnosis may be equivocal, obscure, or absent, or because certain symptoms suggesting a psychoneurotic, affective, or an organic psychosis may also be present. Nevertheless, clinical experience suggests the inclusion of the case in a certain diagnostic category. Psychiatry, by its very nature, abounds in such cases. Schizophrenia has a large area of borderline cases, variously designated as *latent, ambulatory, schizo-affective, borderline, pseudoneurotic,* etc. A less confusing and more accurately descriptive term is *atypical,* and this word will be used hereafter to designate such cases.

In general, these cases, if carefully observed, show Bleuler's primary symptoms—fragmentation of thought, affective disturbance, and ambivalence—in attenuated and often difficult to recognize forms, except perhaps at intervals when they appear more clearly. The secondary symptoms do not as a rule appear. Prominent in these cases are admixtures of classical neurotic—hysterical and phobic—symptoms and psychopathic behavior. Such cases are easily confused with typical psychoneuroses. They are mostly ambulatory, do not deteriorate, and do not show appreciable improvement under any form of treatment or regime. They undoubtedly exist in great numbers and must form a formidable proportion of private practice and outpatient therapeutic failures. The diagnosis of these and other atypical, as well as frank, cases of schizophrenia is based on accurate observation and description of signs, symptoms, and course.

Current Trends in Classification

The concept of atypical or borderline schizophrenia is, as are borderline cases in any field of medicine, a valid concept, provided the cases are viewed with reference to descriptive standards which are widely accepted and of proved usefulness. Some psychiatrists, however, using highly personal interpretations of the meaning of schizophrenia, prefer to go further, and rather than diagnose some cases as schizophrenia and others as borderline cases, they expand the concept to include a large part of all mental disease. A French psychiatrist has even said, "All is schizophrenia." It need hardly be said that, until we know a great deal more about schizophrenia, such a statement is essentially meaningless. The expansion of the term *schizophrenia,* however, is a matter for debate and is largely a matter of personal preference, at the present time.

There is also an opposite tendency to limit or eliminate the use of the term. This tendency is based, not so much on psychodynamic grounds, as on the grounds that the term produces a sense of discouragement in the patient and his relatives. Such a restriction would doubtless be useless, in the long run, for if the term were limited or eliminated, some other term would surely have to be invented to replace it, and this in time would come to have the same connotations as the original.

The term *schizophrenia* has come to have a definite meaning for the entire medical profession, and even, in recent years, for laymen. It certainly refers to a real condition which exists in nature, little as we may know of its origins. It would be better for all of us, professional and layman alike, to face the facts of schizophrenia squarely, rather than to try to avoid them by changing the name of the disorder.

As we know, in many cases the facts are not hard to bear and, indeed, are often easier to deal with than the facts of certain so-called benign or neurotic disturbances.

The demand that all mental disease be lumped into one great category assumes that our categories of diseases are not presently clear-cut and that it is more accurate and useful not to try to distinguish subgroups of mental disease. That this assumption is not true we hope all will agree. Schizophrenia is mostly distinguishable, in descriptive terms, from manic-depressive disease or neurosis, even though it is frequently mixed with neurotic and depressive symptoms of all kinds. It would be a step backward, scientifically speaking, to give up diagnosis just because our present categories are less distinct than we would like. Where classification is absent or weak, science itself may be said to be weak, and certainly psychiatric science is not more weak today than it was in the time of Kraepelin and Bleuler.

A Note of Optimism

In spite of the distress which the term *schizophrenia* may in some circumstances cause laymen, a note of optimism unquestionably colors our professional approach to the theory and treatment of the disorder today. This optimism is based on two important considerations. One, careful observation over the past fifty years has shown us that a large number of schizophrenics appear to make a virtually complete recovery, and in any case are not doomed to continuing deterioration. Second, we live in an era of optimism with regard to almost all matters pertaining to human health and welfare. This optimism is derived in part from the continuing good results which have come from the expansion of the natural sciences during the past two centuries. Medical science has produced such measures as the antibiotics and various other chemotherapies, cardiac surgery, etc., and such important diagnostic aids as the electroencephalograph and the electrocardiograph. Everything seems possible now, including the discovery of the true nature and cure of schizophrenia.

Such an atmosphere of optimism cannot help but have important effects on both therapeutic efforts and research activity in psychiatry. These efforts, perhaps especially the efforts to establish a psychological cause and treatment for schizophrenia and other mental disease, have resulted in a more individualistic, more humanitarian approach to the mentally ill. The art of medicine has been applied with increasing enthusiasm to the mentally sick in the past fifty years, and no one would deny the ethics or the usefulness of this trend.

A recent resurgence of interest and experimentation on a high scale in the neurochemical, neurophysiological, and neuropharmacological aspects of mental disease was stimulated by the development of the tranquilizing drugs. Many hope that the day will come when something like serotonin, adrenaline metabolism, synaptic inhibition, or some similar biochemical problem will provide an explanation for the clinical phenomena of schizophrenia. In the meantime, research activities and the pharmacotherapy already made possible have had important results in helping the social recovery of a large number of schizophrenics and have undoubtedly had an effect on the increasingly rapid turnover of patients in mental hospitals.

Present Approaches

Present attempts to discover the nature of schizophrenia pursue the same lines as in the past, but with vital shifts in emphasis.

Psychodynamic studies along more or less Freudian lines continue on a large scale. Ego development, interpersonal relations in general, and the nuances of family relations in particular are being extensively investigated. Psychobiological studies along Meyerian lines are also being carried on. Many still hold to the belief that the answer to schizophrenia will be found in the realm of psychological knowledge.

Straightforward anatomical research is no longer common, but the biological approach is producing an avalanche of studies in neurochemistry, neurophysiology, and neuropharmacology. The new terms *ataractic, tranquilizer,* and *psychotomimetic drug* have entered our vocabulary, all within the last five or six years. Model or experimental psychoses (with the use of LSD-25 and mescaline) have been experienced by professional researchers themselves who a few years ago would not have dreamed of the possibility of an experimentally induced "break with reality." Thus there has been revived interest in the biological bases of schizophrenia, an interest which had long languished in the shadow of the prestige of psychological approaches.

There are, in addition, studies on the genetic aspects of schizophrenia, and it is our feeling that psychiatrists are presently somewhat more inclined to face the possibility of hereditary factors in schizophrenia without losing their therapeutic optimism.

Finally, we are seeing the development of better statistical methods, not only in hospitals, but also in epidemiological investigations of whole communities and of their constituent groups.

Conclusions

The answer to the question "What is schizophrenia?" in the form of more solid knowledge than we already have may well come from the many research programs now being undertaken all over the world. If we are fortunate enough to come up with discoveries of a public nature which are verifiable by qualified experts of all shades of opinion, we shall be able to expand our definition of *schizophrenia* beyond the present limitations of empirical observation and description. When such knowledge becomes available, we shall have reached the happy position of being able to offer more precise and certain programs for the treatment, control, and prevention of the disease. In the meantime, let us not forget the tools which have served us so well in our time of need—the tools of observation and description and the diagnosis based upon them.

In some future time, hopefully in the not too distant future, we may ask again, "What is schizophrenia?" and answer not only with a description of signs and symptoms, but also with an explanation of the nature of the disease which many consider to be the worst scourge of mankind yet remaining to be conquered by the science which has contributed so much to human health and happiness.

2

Neurophysiological Contributions to the Understanding of Schizophrenia

FREDERIC G. WORDEN [1]

Introduction

There is no neurophysiological contribution to the understanding of schizophrenia. Some information (7, 9, 14, 18, 19, 31, 48) has been obtained about central neural processes in patients labeled *schizophrenic,* but its meaning, neurophysiologically, is not clear because not enough is known of normal brain function. From the clinical side, further uncertainty is introduced by the word *schizophrenia* because the terms used to denote categories of mental illness continue to pose grave conceptual and practical problems. Indeed, competent clinicians have stated recently "There are no natural mental disease entities" (40). They propose a unitary concept of mental illness and health and suggest that no further effort be made to separate schizophrenia from other types of mental illness. This provides a convenient

[1] Associate Research Psychiatrist and Associate Professor of Psychiatry, Department of Psychiatry, University of California School of Medicine, Los Angeles, and the Veterans Administration Hospital, Long Beach, California.
This work was supported by USPHS Mental Health Career Investigator Grant (M1169) and by grants from the Ford Foundation and the USPHS (B611).

bridge leading to the central purpose of this report, which is to show that there is now reason to expect a breakthrough of knowledge about the neural processes underlying mental health and mental illness. Emphasis will here be placed on two somewhat different experimental programs, both of which involve recent experimental and conceptual approaches to questions concerning brain function and behavioral phenomena: (1) some trends revealed in current Russian scientific reports will be summarized; and (2) some developments in Western neurophysiology will be illustrated by reporting briefly on a project from our own laboratories.

Recent Russian Literature

The National Medical Library has supplied medical schools throughout the United States and Canada with two volumes containing English translations of 75 selected Russian articles on the central nervous system and behavior (51). These were prepared as background material for participants in the first Josiah Macy, Jr. Conference on the central nervous system and behavior.

Twenty-two problems in all areas of medical research are listed by the Academy of Medical Sciences, USSR, for the sixth 5-year plan, 1956–1960. Of these, the first two are "Physiology and Pathology of Higher Nervous Activity" and "Basic Mechanisms of Activity of the Nervous System and Their Role in Regulating the Function of the Organism." Listed later is the topic "Problems of Clinical Neurology." Extensive details are given under these titles, which are exciting and in some ways unique to the Western reader.

Since Ivan Pavlov, the Russians have developed the doctrine of "neural trophicity" so that it now constitutes a major realm (10) of investigative techniques and accumulated data. Concerning trophic functions of the nervous system, Pavlov said in 1920: "Every organ is controlled by three kinds of nerves: functional nerves which set off or arrest its functional activity (contraction of a muscle, secretion of a gland, etc.); vascular nerves (which regulate the gross supply of chemical material and removal of waste) in the form of a certain amount of blood inflow to the organ; trophic nerves which determine to the best advantage of the entire organism as a whole the precise extent of the final utilization of these materials by every organ." This triple system of nervous influence is conceived as follows: "nervous impulses which originate in one group of nerve cells not only stimulate other neurons, inducing therein nervous impulses, but at the same time, act also upon the entire trophicity of these neurons—that is, on all the conditions of the inflow to the tissues of nutrient substances and oxygen—the conditions of transfer of these substances from the blood of the capillaries to the intercellular space—their assimilation by the nerve cells and on the metabolism within these cells." This concept has led to many studies of the relationships between cellular respiration, central nervous activity, and various factors influencing the organism.

The Russians have addressed themselves especially to individual links in processes of cellular respiration in tissues and organs of an integral animal. They feel that summary studies of the respiration of isolated tissues in the Warburg apparatus are inadequate because (1) changes in individual stages of respiratory processes may balance out and not reflect themselves in the total respiratory resultant, (2) the isolated tissue is no longer subject to trophic influences on cellular respiration exerted by the nervous system of the intact organism. Applying such an approach to the study of gastritis induced in cats, they have shown that changes occur not only in the mucous membranes of the stomach, liver, and intestines, but also within the metabolism of the brain where the anoxidative link of cellular respiration was found to be depressed. Another study showed that vitamin D, in addition to its role in phosphorus-calcium metabolism, has a connection with cellular respiration in various organs, especially the brain, and this was felt to relate to psychic retardation occurring in children with rickets and to certain central nervous system disturbances occurring in the arctic polar night where insufficient vitamin D_3 (cholecalciferol) is formed from the skin. From other studies they have concluded that the sympathetic nervous system does not act on cellular respiration, but rather on carbohydrate metabolism and the circulation of nutrients available for cellular respiration. Adrenaline (epinephrine) has been shown to decrease rather than to increase processes of cellular respiration in muscles, brain, heart, and the mucous membrane of the stomach. Many studies are reported which show the effect on cellular respiration within various organs produced by physiologic, pharmocologic, and pathogenic factors. The Russians view these findings concerning neural trophicity as the link connecting the role of the nervous system and the role of metabolism in the life of organisms.

Another idea of Pavlov's, the concept of *interoception,* has been developed experimentally by the Russians. In 1930 Pavlov said, "But detailed higher analysis and synthesis carried out by the cerebral hemispheres is not limited to the external world. The inner world of the organism, organic changes taking place in it, is subjected to the same analysis and synthesis" (11). This theory led to the creation of techniques for demonstrating receptors in internal organs (1). For example, an organ, such as the kidney, uterus, or a piece of stomach or intestine, is isolated from the general circulation and perfused, leaving intact only its neural connection with the rest of the animal. Stimuli are then applied to the isolated organ and the effects on various aspects of the organism can be observed. Receptors sensitive to mechanical, physical, or chemical stimuli have been demonstrated in a variety of internal organs and are assumed to exist in all tissues. By using conditioning techniques it has been shown that these internal stimuli, just like those from the external world, can acquire the power to elicit conditioned responses (2) such as salivation or paw-lifting. Internal signals differ from external signals in that they have a differential strength regarding various organs. For example, distention of the bladder forms a faster and stronger connection when it is used as the signal for a conditioned leg flexion than when it is used as the conditioned stimulus for a salivary response.

That signals from internal organs are differentiated has been widely demonstrated, and the nature and limits of differentiation have been explored (2). For example, a dog with an isolated segment of the ileocecal gut was conditioned so that a leg flexion and respiratory changes were elicited by a stimulus applied to one side of the ileocecal valve, while the same stimulus applied on the other side of the ileocecal valve elicited an inhibitory reflex. This differentiation was clear even though the points of stimulation were less than 2 centimeters apart. In similar experiments two thermal stimuli applied to a bit of stomach and two tactile stimuli applied to the uterus were clearly differentiated.

In another type of study the signals from internal organs have been shown to exert temporary or prolonged effects on higher nervous activity concerned with learning (3). Here, a typical method is to establish a variety of conditioned responses to external stimuli, such as buzzers, lights, etc. Then an isolated bit of the animal's viscera is stimulated and the effect on the externally established conditioned reflexes is measured. In more complex experiments, conditioned responses are established to both internal and external signals, so that interactions between them can be revealed. For example, by pairing it with shock to the paw, an internal stimulus acquires the power to elicit a leg flexion in the dog. At the same time an auditory signal is paired with food until a conditioned salivary response is established. It was then found that the conditioned salivary response to the external signal was severely inhibited by a preceding visceral signal, even when the visceral signal had lost its capacity to produce leg flexion or any visible change in the dog's behavior. That is, the visceral stimulus continued to exert a hidden central influence even when its conditioned motor response failed to appear.

In other studies, complex chains of conditioned reflexes are established. A dog is taught to lift his paw in response to a 1-per-second inflation of intestinal segment. In a second stage which does not involve any further intestinal stimulation, passive paw-lifting is used as the signal for a conditioned salivary reflex. If now, the intestinal stimulus alone is applied, it elicits first a paw-lifting then a salivary response.

In their experimental approach to the question of stimuli from internal organs the Russians have not neglected variables which are characteristically emphasized in Pavlovian theory. One of these is the nervous balance or temperament of the experimental animal as delineated by responses to conditioning procedures and indices of vegetative function. Differences in phenomena concerning internal signals are frequently correlated with differences in the types of nervous balance of the animal subjects (2). Another variable is the background state of the organ under study, so that, for example, the effect of stimulating the resting uterus has been shown to be very different from the effect of stimulating the gestating uterus (2). A third variable influencing the effects of internal stimuli is the current functional state of the central nervous system. This has been beautifully demonstrated in a series of experiments derived from the concept of "hysteriosis" (4). It had been shown that if the left tibial nerve of a dog is tetanized for several hours it loses its capacity to give a response, but paradoxically, a marked lowering of threshold of excitability develops in the contralateral (right) tibial nerve. This was called *hysteriosis* because it seemed related phenomenologically and conceptually to hysteria. When this procedure was applied to studies of the effects of signals from internal organs, it was found that they were extremely sensitive to states of hysteriosis. For example, a mild distention of an isolated segment of intestine is found to have little effect on blood pressure, pulse, respiration, etc. If, however, the tibial nerve is tetanized for 2 or 3 hours, then the same mild inflation produces an effect so powerful that it can be fatal for the animal. By applying Novocain to the isolated intestinal segment the effect is abolished, indicating that it is a neural reflex mechanism. Similar results, using other organs and other stimuli, have led to the conclusion that the effect of a signal from an internal organ is highly dependent on the functional state of the brain which receives the signals.

Internal signals have also been studied in man (5). In one study a "manometer," which the patient thought was indicating intrabladder pressure, was manipulated in association with the introduction of fluid into the bladder through catheters. Through this conditioning procedure the manipulations of the "manometer" by the experimenters became a conditioned visual stimulus which could elicit the subjective need to urinate, associated with contraction of the bladder, and changes in pulse rate, blood pressure, and galvanic skin response. These conditioned bladder reflexes were dissociated from the actual volume of fluid in the bladder, occurring instead in connection with the visual stimulus (the movements of the indicator needle on the dial of the "manometer").

The complex multitude of processes from internal and external worlds is conceived by the Russians to be analyzed and synthesized in the cortex: "all these meet each other, collide, interact; the cerebral cortex with its processes of excitation and inhibition, refined analysis, and dissected synthesis receiving them variously in their plurality, produces a limited and homogeneous resultant." This resultant is termed a *dynamic stereotype* and represents a classified and balanced arrangement of all the conditioned and unconditioned processes reflected in the cortex (6).

Pavlov's concepts of cortical excitation and inhibition have, of course, received much experimental attention (28). Neurophysiological techniques, such as electrical recording, have been applied but will not be reported here. They have, however, employed conditioning techniques which are unusually interesting. One preparation, for example, involves externalizing symmetrical areas of the rear third of the dog's tongue, leaving intact the neural innervation. In such an animal, weak acid to the externalized bits of tongue gives a salivary reflex just as if the acid were placed in the mouth, but with the difference that the response is unilateral. Acid applied to the right segment of tongue elicits saliva from the right parotid, and vice versa. With this preparation, a conditioning procedure was established in which an auditory signal was paired with acid stimulation, first to the left tongue segment for 10 seconds, followed by stimulation for 10 seconds to the right tongue segment. Gradually a conditioned salivary reflex developed, first from the left parotid gland, the same side as the side of the tongue which was being stimulated first. With further training, a bilateral response developed, but the left response remained always greater than the right. When this conditioned response was fully established and stabilized, then the experimenter reversed the order of stimulation, so that now the *right* side of the tongue was stimulated for 10 seconds, followed by stimulation for 10 seconds to the left side of the tongue. At first, secretion from the left parotid continued to predominate, even though the right tongue was now receiving the first stimulation. Shortly, however, the conditioned responses diminished bilaterally, and then, after several days, the dog suffered a severe nervous disorder manifested by continuous secretion from both salivary glands, uneasiness, and other neurotic symptoms, so that it could not be used for further training. It should be noted that both sides of the tongue were always stimulated, only the temporal order being changed, and that the dog was not being asked to discriminate between a reward-punishment or a go-no-go type of situation. As the authors assume, it seems unlikely that the dog cared which side of his tongue was stimulated first or which parotid gland was producing the most saliva. They account for the neurotic breakdown in terms of processes or cortical excitation and inhibition. It would appear that this experiment is of considerable theoretical interest, since it does not lend itself gracefully to interpretation in the usual forms of psychological-conflict theory.

Complex sequential behaviors in a relatively free-moving type of situation have also been investigated by conditioning techniques. A dog is trained to approach a lamp on a support and lick it, whereupon the experimenter turns on the lamp. The dog then goes to a rug in another part of the room and stands on it. Standing on the rug, he must look in the direction of a nonvisible metronome. When he does so, the experimenter turns on the metronome, and the dog then moves to another part of the room and jumps on a table, there to receive food.

After this cycle of behavior is established, then the experimenter introduces an extraneous signal, a rattling noise. If this is introduced while the dog is standing on the rug looking at the metronome, then the dog immediately jumps to the table in the absence of the metronome sound; this is interpreted as being due to the fact that preparatory cortical excitation is so strong at this stage that the sound of the rattle releases the action. If, however, the rattling noise is given after the dog licks the lamp and is on his way to the rug, then the dog gives a strong orientation reflex. That is, he stops for 3–5 seconds, looks in the direction of the rattling noise, but then continues toward the rug to complete the cycle in his usual fashion. But when the rattle is given at the beginning, as the dog goes to the support but before he licks the lamp, then not only is the licking act inhibited, but the entire cycle is inhibited. Moreover, some dogs refuse to lick the lamp for several days even when hungry, and one dog showed a disturbance in behavior that lasted 10 days and another developed a permanent neurosis. This is interpreted: "Thus we see that the neural processes in various phases of the elaborated cycle of activity have a diverse structure, diverse resistance and intensity—of themselves; the motor acts when the dog goes to the rug and to the support are quite identical. However, the application of rattling during one such act leads only to their brief retardation and during another, can lead to a neural disturbance. It is clear that we have to do with a united activity and united neural processes, which in one phase of this activity, possess other properties than in another phase."

In concluding these brief excerpts from the Russian literature, three points should be made: In the first place, it should be noted that no effort has been made here to evaluate the validity of the results. I have neither sufficient first-hand knowledge of the Russian investigators and their scientific standards nor competence in many of the fields involved in these reports. In the second place, assuming that the value of Russian scientific writings are somewhat comparable to scientific reports in general, it would appear that, from the beginning, the Pavlovian concepts have fostered the development of experimental programs which have been more multidisciplinary and more geared to the organism as a whole than experimental approaches in the Western world. Pavlovian experiments encompass to an unusual extent the personality characteristics of the animal, the background states of individual organs, and the relationships between signals from the inside and the outside world to ongoing behavioral, metabolic, endocrinological, and neural processes. Elsewhere (13, 47) it has been suggested that Pavlov stultified the growth of Russian psychology, but this criticism should be qualified. Pavlov abandoned psychological terms and concepts in favor of speculative pseudoneurology, but he never gave up observing psychological phenomena in the context of the biological processes of his animals. His followers have brought the earlier pseudoneurology into closer connection with neurological facts and have enlarged the scope and complexity of psychological phenomena explored by their uniquely psychobiological approach. Freud, a Western counterpart of Pavlov, sacrificed his neurological studies in order to concentrate on psychological phenomena, perhaps thereby contributing to the fact that Western neurological and psychological disciplines have been so widely separated in techniques, terms, and concepts. These differences between Russian and Western scientific development involve advantages and disadvantages for both sides, but, more importantly, they suggest that the data of the two sides could be advantageously put together. The third point in regard to the Russian work is that the data given in the two volumes of translations concern areas not extensively studied experimentally in the West, such as neural influences on cellular respiration, signals from internal organs, and the organization of complex conditioned behaviors. Although the Russian findings are generally quite consonant with clinical psychiatric findings in the West, it seems very significant that the Russians have developed experimental approaches to such problems, thereby clarifying and validating many clinical assumptions and opening the way for further progress.

Neurophysiological Approaches to Behavior in Western Science

Western science has in recent years developed an experimental approach which is contributing new knowledge about the neurophysiological correlates of phenomena which have traditionally been studied mostly in their psychological aspects. The past two decades have seen the most exciting and promising progress in the entire history of man's effort to understand how his brain and mind are related. A survey of these events is not attempted here, but a few comments which can serve as background for a brief description of a research program from our own laboratories will be set forth. The conceptualizations of brain function which led to our project were not available even ten years ago, and our experiments exemplify one type of research approach based upon them. Results from such programs are going to appear increasingly in the scientific periodicals, and perhaps this firsthand account will provide some familiarity with how they are obtained and what they mean.

The brain model of today is so drastically revised from that of twenty years ago that it now resembles its former self less than it does the kind of organ needed to account for the complexities of behavior. The theoretical picture has been revolutionized at all levels, from the microscopic picture of the neuron, through the synapse, and up to the whole brain functioning during behavior. If the older brain model can be said to represent results obtained from part-studies of the anesthetized brain or from relatively crude behavioral approaches employed following ablations of a neural structure, the newer brain picture can be seen to derive from investigations of larger aspects of the unanesthetized brain associated with more adequate methods of assessing and influencing behavior. For our purposes three major factors in this remodeling will be mentioned, and all three depend on these newer methods.

First of all, the older picture of functions rooted geographically in structural centers, with telephonic type of communications to provide interactions between relatively stable and independent centers, has been replaced by a picture in which functional processes are handled by widespread and dynamically changing cell assemblies (20, 29, 30, 32, 52). The structural loci are now regarded as only optimal or prominent contributors rather than as monopolistic sources of functional specialties; and furthermore, parts are considered to function as a whole on a *transactional* (37) rather than an interactional basis. Whereas the interactional notion involved sequential intercommunication between relatively autonomous and unvarying centers, the sum of which represented behavior, the transactional picture involves processes in which the centers themselves change in relation to the whole, thereby acquiring different roles during temporary or prolonged temporospatial patterns of dynamic plasticity and circular systems of reverberation, influenced by local and general feedbacks.

The second element is the discovery (41) and understanding (8, 15, 34, 35, 39) of the functional role of the ascending reticular system. Until the unanesthetized brain was investigated, this system seemed to have no function except to hold the brain together. Now it becomes difficult to imagine a system more appropriate for the transactional type of brain function than this messy, complicated network of neurons and fibers (12, 49) extending throughout the core of the brain stem and thalamus. It receives information, via collaterals, from all the classical afferent (sensory) systems, from cortex and higher centers, and from efferent (effector) systems. *Within* it occur diffuse and local processes involving special and multiple inputs of types appropriate for integrative processes (22, 50), and *from* it modulating influences emerge to act diffusely or focally upon the whole cortical mantle, the whole efferent motor system, and the whole classical system of afferent transmission of sensory information (21, 33, 35). The behavioral implications so far demonstrated include phenomena of sleep-wakefulness, general alertness and directed attention, perceptual speed and accuracy (16), learning, and the extrapyramidal adjustment of motor activity.

The third element has been the advent of a new and more adequate neurophysiological understanding of motivational and emotional processes. A brilliant technical innovation in 1954 (43) made it possible to begin a new exploration of neural structures related to reward and punishment types of motivated behavior. Simply stated, it was found that an animal who can, by pressing a lever, deliver an electrical stimulus to his brain through an implanted electrode, will press the lever at different rates according to the site within his brain which receives the stimulus. To stimulate some sites he will lever-press at incredibly rapid and sustained rates; at other sites he will attempt to escape the situation after one lever press. For some rewarding sites, he will forego food and sleep or run mazes and overcome obstacles in order to stimulate himself via the lever. Furthermore, the lever-pressing response to some sites is sensitive to other drives, so that, for example, manipulations of the intensity of hunger or sex drives will influence the rate of lever pressing (42).

Since 1937 rapid advances in our knowledge of the neural substrates of emotional processes have followed a guess (45) and an experiment (26) both concerning the olfactory brain. Currently, anatomical and physiological knowledge (25, 36, 38, 46, 54) of the rhinencephalon (olfactory brain) reveals that it is intimately connected with the subjective (48, 53), autonomic, and expressive features of emotional processes and that it is perhaps equipped to generate affective values in terms of the past experience of the organism as it relates to current information concerning the external and internal world of the animal (44).

It becomes clear that the current conception of brain function facilitates a form of research activity which overrides the traditional disciplinary barriers. Our project is typical of this trend in that it involves the collaboration of a psychologist, Dr. James T. Marsh,[2] and two psychiatrists, Dr. William J. Hockaday[3] and myself. The hypotheses underlying our work are drawn from the facts and theories of a variety of psychological and neurological disciplines. In our experiments, the neurophysiological technique for electrical recording from the unanesthetized cat by means of chronic electrodes implanted in the brain is combined with techniques from experimental psychology for assessing and influencing behavior. Working in the laboratories of the Veterans Administration Hospital at Long Beach, California, we receive essential assistance and guidance provided by the multidisciplinary group of investigators assembled there under the leadership of Drs. Magoun, French, and Lindsley.

The experiments to be reported here have sought to correlate behavioral states and stages of learning in the cat with electrophysiological events occurring at various levels of the auditory pathway. The existence of such correlates had been suggested by the following observations previously reported by others: (1) If an auditory stimulus is repetitively presented, the cat gradually appears to lose interest in it, and concurrently with this behavioral change there occurs a decrease in the amplitude of electrical responses evoked by the auditory stimulus (23). (2) If now the auditory stimulus is followed by an electric shock to the forepaw, after a few such combinations, the auditory stimulus will, once again, elicit full-sized electrical responses (17). (3) An auditory stimulus which has been paired with shock to the paw will elicit responses from parts of the brain where no electrical

[2] Fellow, Foundations' Fund for Research in Psychiatry and Assistant Professor, Medical Psychology, Department of Psychiatry, University of California School of Medicine, Los Angeles.

[3] Instructor, Department of Psychiatry, University of Louisville School of Medicine. Dr. Hockaday is spending the year at the research laboratories, Long Beach Veterans Administration Hospital and the Department of Anatomy, University of California School of Medicine, Los Angeles.

responses had been evoked prior to the pairing with electric shocks (17). (4) If, while an auditory stimulus is being presented, the cat's attention is captured by another stimulus, such as the sight of live mice in a glass jar or the smell of fish through a rubber tube, then the amplitude of electrical responses evoked by the auditory stimulus shrinks as the cat attends behaviorally to the other stimuli (24). These facts suggest that changes in the significance of an auditory signal or changes in the direction of a cat's attention are reflected in electrophysiological changes.

In an effort to clarify these phenomena, we became interested in the fact that there is, in the unanesthetized animal, a marked variability in the amplitude of potentials evoked by an unvarying stimulus. This variability differs from the previously mentioned changes in amplitudes in that it has a very short time constant, dramatic differences occurring in the amplitudes of two responses evoked by two identical stimuli separated by an interval of 500 milliseconds or less. In order to find out if this variability also correlated with behavioral phenomena, we measured it in samples of evoked responses obtained under three conditions: (1) while the cat was fully anesthetized, (2) while the cat was alert and investigating himself or his surroundings, (3) at various stages of training which established the auditory stimulus as a signal for food reward. For all conditions a standard tone was used having a pitch of 1,200 cycles and a duration of 40 msec. This was presented at a rate of two tones per second, through a loud-speaker to the cat in a soundproof room. In order to add a learned significance to the tones, we designed a remotely operated training apparatus which could be used in the soundproof room to deliver food rewards to the cat. Fig. 2–1 shows this apparatus. Note the food box with levers attached. The hungry cat can see and smell a dish of food in the box through holes in the lid, but he cannot eat until he presses one of the levers which activate the motor to open the lid.

Fig. 2–1. Training apparatus. Note food box with levers, sliding perforated lid, and linkage to motor.

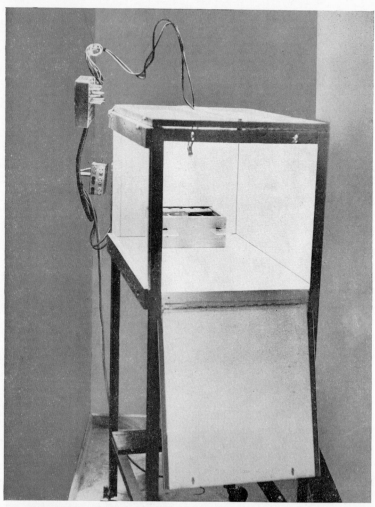

Fig. 2–2. Training apparatus in soundproof room. Note cable for connecting animal to records.

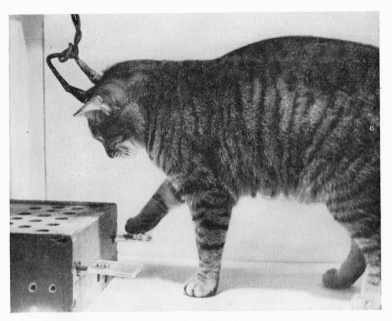

Fig. 2–3. Cat responding in training apparatus.

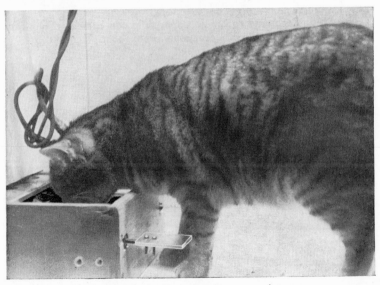

Fig. 2–4. Cat receiving reward.

Fig. 2–5. Recording room. At upper right can be seen a one-way window opening into the adjacent soundproof room.

Fig. 2–2 shows the apparatus in place. Note the plug and cable through which electrodes in the cat's head are connected with recording apparatus in another room.

In Fig. 2–3 a cat is pressing one of the pedals. In these experiments we used just one pedal and one tone pitch. Each training trial consists of turning on the 2-per-second tone for 20 seconds, during which a lever pressed by the cat will shut off the tones and open the food box for approximately 4 seconds. During silent intervals between trials the lever is inactivated. Each daily training session consists of twenty-five trials with silent intervals such that a session lasts about 30 minutes. Under such conditions cats learn to lever-press successfully enough to obtain about half a can of cat food. Electric counters record the number of successful responses (lever-presses during the tones) and the number of unsuccessful lever-presses occurring during silent intervals, and the number of trials where no lever-press occurred during the tones can be calculated. Fig. 2–4 shows the cat receiving his reward. After one or two experiences cats learn to withdraw their heads before the lid closes.

Fig. 2–5 shows the adjacent recording room. A one-way observation window opens into the soundproof room. A 14-channel photographically recording oscillograph is connected in parallel with the EEG pens in such fashion that we can monitor with the EEG and simultaneously obtain oscillographic records. Our measurements are made on the oscillographic rather than by ink-written records. A dual-beam oscilloscope is used as a visual monitor. Also shown in the figure are a timer and power supply, which, in conjunction with oscillators and amplifiers, produce the sequences of tones and activate the levers so that they will open the food box only while tones are on. One great difficulty in this kind of research is to obtain adequate and accurately timed behavioral observations. A dictating machine is connected so that whenever a behavioral note is dictated, an artifact is produced in one channel of the record. In this way it is

AUDITORY RESPONSE AMPLITUDE & VARIABILITY
UNDER VARIOUS BEHAVIORAL CONDITIONS
(cat: mother)

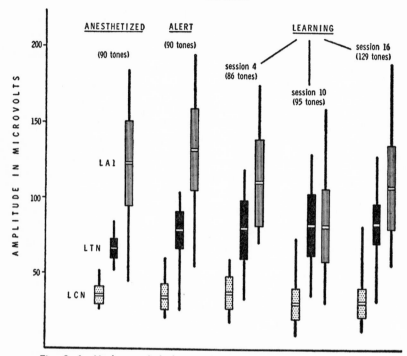

Fig. 2–6. Under each behavioral condition are three vertical bars representing response samples obtained from left cochlear nucleus (LCN), left trapezoid nucleus (LTN), and left auditory cortex (LAI). Mean amplitude of samples is shown as clear area in center of wide bar which shows one standard deviation on each side of the mean. Range is shown by thin black line.

possible, after an experiment, to play back the dictated record and annotate the artifacts on the EEG.

Turning now to some data, Fig. 2–6 presents them in graphic form. Across the top are listed three behavioral conditions: *anesthetized, alert,* and *learning.* The three subtitles under learning refer to different stages of training, an early sample, an intermediate sample, and a still later sample.

Along the vertical axis is a scale of microvolts, our recording equipment being calibrated so that amplitudes can be measured in microvolts. Peak-to-peak measurements of responses are made, using an arbitrary time boundary to avoid problems of interpreting the temporal limits of response components. Evoked potentials from three auditory centers are presented in the form of three vertical bars under each behavioral title. The first dotted bar is the *cochlear nucleus;* the black bar is the *nucleus of the trapezoid body,* and the stripped bar is *primary auditory cortex,* all in the left side of the cat. (Labels are tentative since electrode locations are not yet histologically confirmed.) The mean amplitude of each sample is shown as a clear central area; the standard deviation is shown by the wider band; and the range is shown by the ends of the black line. It can be seen that in the subcortical relays (the first two bars in each group) the variability increases from anesthetized to alert, from alert to early learning, and then, in later learning it appears to decrease. The extreme range, on the other hand, tends to increase progressively. Note also that variability is greater and increases more in the higher (trapezoid) nucleus than in the lower (cochlear) nucleus. The cortical samples show no consistent trend, a fact which we believe reflects the operation of other variables. We are conducting further experiments to see if this can be clarified.

Statistical testing of these results indicates that the differences in variability from anesthetized to alert and from alert to learning are significant (p less than .001), but the difference between early and later learning is not significant. Experiments are in progress to see if a significant decrease in variability occurs as learning is established over a longer time. At present it can be said that electrical potentials evoked in subcortical auditory relays by an unvarying auditory stimulus show the least variability under anesthesia, more when the animal is alert, and even more as the animal is taught to respond to the auditory stimulus as a signal. Further, it appears that the higher auditory relays show more variability, or plasticity, than do the lower ones. The fact that the extremes of variation in amplitude increase progressively, while the means do not, reflects the fact that amplitudes become very large at some times but are also frequently extremely small.

In order to give an impressionistic view of further possibilities in this type of experimental program, some multichannel ink-written records are shown in Figs. 2–7 through 2–10. These were obtained from the same cat at various times: before, during, and after the animal had learned to respond correctly to the auditory signal. The location and amplification of the various channels remain the same in all the records. The names assigned to the channels are not histologically confirmed, since this animal is still alive and in training.

In Fig. 2–7 it can be seen that the evoked potentials in various auditory relays begin to show an increase in amplitude only after the cat begins to press the lever in association with the auditory signal.

In Fig. 2–8 it can be seen that as the training is continued and the cat's behavior becomes more connected with the auditory signal, there is a progressive spread of the large-amplitude electrical responses, with the trace labeled LCN being included in this only in the last record of Fig. 2–8. In passing it might be mentioned that, unlike a telephone system, the auditory afferent system shows differential plasticity at different levels, so that one stimulus may evoke small responses in some levels and large responses at other levels, while the next identical stimulus may evoke a reversed spatial display of local inhibitions and facilitations. Thus, in Fig. 2–8, it is not unusual that in the middle record all responses are large except that of LCN, which is at the input end of the system.

Fig. 2–9 shows one continuous record taken at a much later stage of training. The EEG picture shows a marked change from the generalized large amplitudes of Fig. 2–8. In Fig. 2–9 there are episodes of both large and small amplitude responses which occur in association with transient behavioral phenomena observed during the trial. Another difference is that in Fig. 2–8 all the leads eventually showed large responses, whereas in Fig. 2–9 it can be seen that different neural loci are showing amplitude changes at different times.

Fig. 2–10 shows a record also taken on the sixteenth day of training and only five trials later than the record shown in Fig. 2–9. Here again is a very different EEG picture. Correlations between electrical and behavioral phenomena are far less easy to see, since the patterns are more temporospatially spread out.

The differences between Fig. 2–9 and Fig. 2–10 illustrate one problem concerning the evaluation of these experiments and other research programs concerned with central neural phenomena related to psychological processes. In the first place, as is well known clinically, very different states of mind can underlie actions which are externally similar. Anthropomorphically, we could speculate that the last two figures differ because the cat's state of mind when he pressed the lever in one was different from that when he pressed it in the other. At least, electrophysiologically, his brain functioned differently during the two similar behaviors. In our experience, this kind of difference is characteristic of this kind of experiment and demands a search for other variables.

These variables include psychological processes which may not be directly observable, such as changes in motivation, perception, emotion, and attention. From cat to cat there are striking differences in personality, presumably related to inherent and experimental factors. Furthermore, many variables are involved in such matters as training pro-

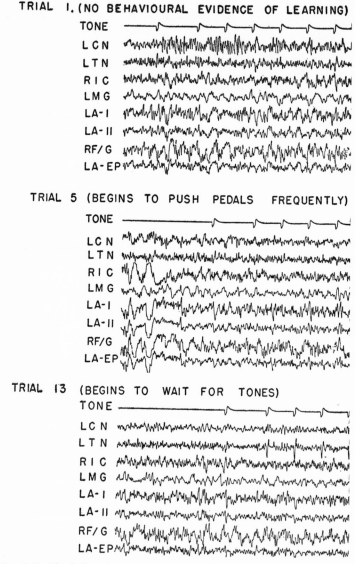

Fig. 2–7. Third day of training. In each record, the top trace is a signal indicating the auditory stimulus presentation, a 2-per-second tone, of 40-msec duration, at a pitch of 1,200 cycles per second. Abbreviations used in this and subsequent figures: LCN, left cochlear nucleus; LTN, left trapezoid nucleus; RIE, right inferior collicules; LMG, left medial geniculate; LA-I, left auditory cortex, primary; LA-II, left auditory cortex, secondary; RF/G, reticular formation; LA-EP, left auditory cortex Ep.

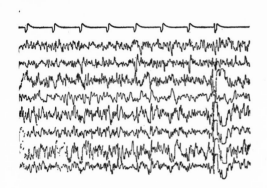

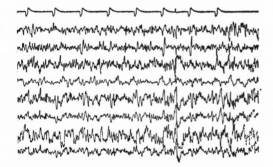

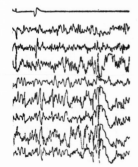

Trial 1 was taken before any behavioral evidence of learning and resembles central records taken before training was started.

Trial 5 was taken after cat learned to operate pedal efficiently, but before pedal-pressing showed evidence of being related to auditory stimuli.

Trial 13 was taken shortly after the cat began to show a tendency to wait for the auditory signal before pressing the pedal. Note the increased amplitude of the responses of LTN.

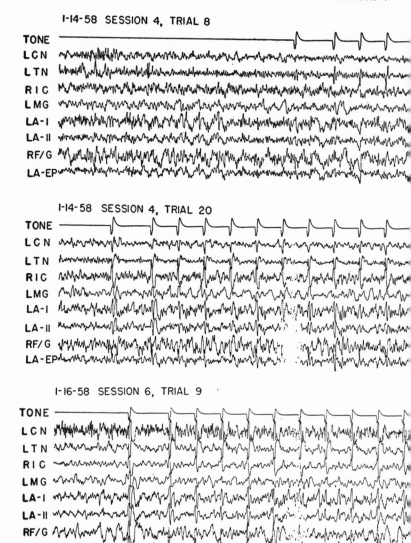

Fig. 2–8. Fourth and sixth day of training. The two top records are from the fourth day of training; the bottom record is from the sixth day. Note that the progressive increase in amplitude of evoked potentials does not include

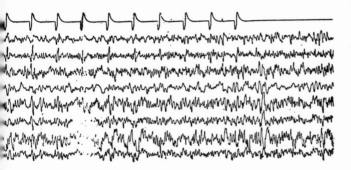

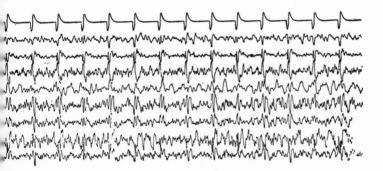

GAP IN RECORD = 5"

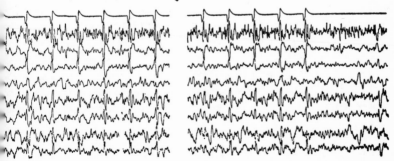

LCN until the bottom record. This EEG picture is unlike anything seen in this cat during months of pretraining experiments which involved recording the responses to the same auditory stimulus.

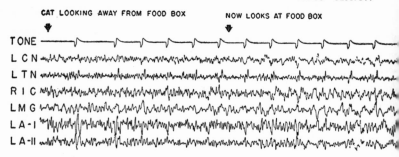

CAT LOOKING AWAY FROM FOOD BOX   NOW LOOKS AT FOOD BOX

TONE
L C N
L T N
R I C
L M G
L A-I
L A-II

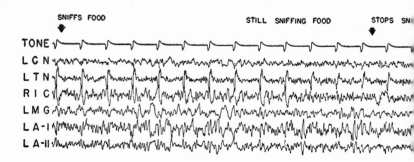

SNIFFS FOOD   STILL SNIFFING FOOD   STOPS SN

TONE
L C N
L T N
R I C
L M G
L A-I
L A-II

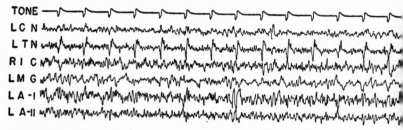

MOVES TO LEFT PEDAL

TONE
L C N
L T N
R I C
L M G
L A-I
L A-II

Fig. 2–9. Sixteenth day of training. This is one continuous record of Trial 17 on the sixteenth day of training. Accurately timed behavioral notes are shown across the top. The cat was looking away from the food box when the tones came on, and as he looks toward the food box, and then sniffs the food, there is a build-up of amplitude of the electrical responses. As he looks away again, the evoked potentials become small in amplitude, but again build up as he looks back, moves to the pedal, and finally presses the pedal. Eighty-

STILL LOOKING AT FOOD BOX   BUT SITTING DOWN

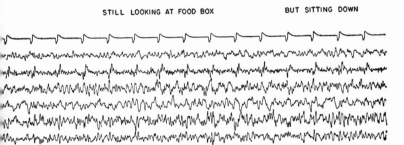

LOOKS AWAY   LOOKS BACK

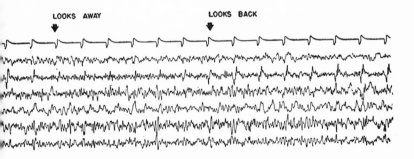

LOOKING INTENTLY AT FOOD BOX   PUSHES RIGHT PEDAL

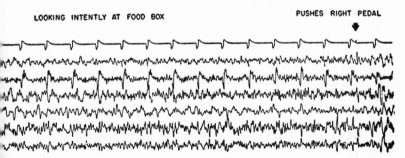

eight tones occur (equal to 44 seconds) before the lever press, and this long-response latency is probably related to the fact that this was a late trial in the day's session and the cat had already been rewarded with a considerable amount of food.

In contrast to earlier training shown in Fig. 2–8, the picture here is of particular episodes of large and small amplitudes associated with transient behavioral events, not generalized large amplitudes.

AUDITORY   RESPONSES

SESSION   16,   TRI

LOOKS AT FOOD BOX

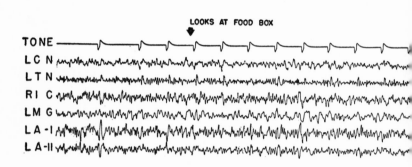

LOOKING   INTENTLY

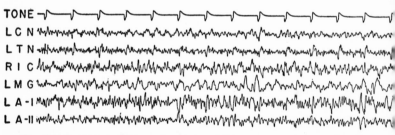

Fig. 2–10. Sixteenth day of training. This is a record taken 5 trials after that shown in Fig. 2–9. Unlike Fig. 2–9, this record shows far less clear-cut and simple correlations between behavioral and electrical phenomena. For example, note that LTN does not build up until

cedures, experimental settings, electrode placements, and recording techniques. Just in terms of time alone, these are formidable problems. For example, although some of our results seem very promising and exciting, we do not yet know how long it will take to complete sufficient experiments on a number of cats that some general conclusions can be

RING   LEARNING

(2-3-58)

STILL LOOKING AT FOOD BOX

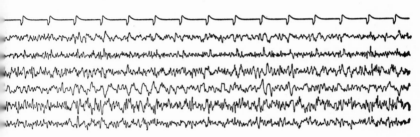

BOX   MOVES TO FOOD BOX   PUSHES RIGHT PEDAL

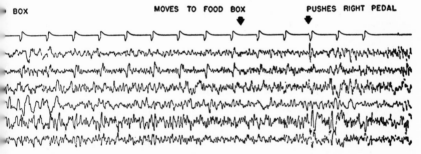

relatively late in the trial, and that LA-I in the bottom section of record builds up as the cat looks intently at the food box, only to shrink down as the cat moves to the food box and pushes the lever.

achieved. We feel that the temptation to oversimplify the really complex processes occurring even in a cat's head and behavior must be avoided, since it does not seem possible to judge results unless data are obtained concerning how much phenomena vary as identical experiments are repeatedly conducted, what kind of sampling procedures have been used, and what statistical probabilities are involved. These problems, so familiar in psychological and psychiatric work, are becoming more and more important in animal studies where neurophysiological and psychological observations are made of complex phenomena. Nevertheless, the experimental methods now possible with animals do offer considerable hope that a basic knowledge of the neural processes related to psychologically observed phenomena can be established and extended. Such a basic science of brain function and behavior should certainly be a contribution to the understanding of mental illnesses and mental health. As to the nature of the contribution, this question is considered extensively in a volume reporting two recent conferences on integrating the approaches to mental illness (27). In these conferences, a violin was introduced into the discussion of organic and psychological approaches, the issue being put in terms of either studying the structure and vibration of the violin or of listening to the sonata. Let me suggest that the hope for research progress, as expressed here, is based on the increasing capacity of man to study the structure and vibrations of the violin while simultaneously listening to the music. This does not mean reductionism, for psychological facts seem to be as basic as any other, and, for example, the color red, as an experience, will remain also an experience even if its molecular biological substrate is fully discovered and understood.

Discussion

JULES H. MASSERMAN [4]

Dr. Worden begins his essay with the disarming comment: "There is *no* neurophysiological contribution to the understanding of schizophrenia," and thus spares us from

[4] Professor of Neurology and Psychiatry, Department of Psychiatry, The Medical School, Northwestern University, Chicago.

dealing directly with that controversial if not altogether dubious syndrome. Instead, he proceeds to a discussion of seven categories of Soviet experiments which, in brief review, can be commented on with corresponding brevity as follows:

1. Our Soviet colleagues report that the brain is subject to variations in body metabolism and can in turn influence the latter. One could hardly disagree with this observation, though the postulate of special cerebral "trophic nerves" is open to question.

2. Russian Laikas, like their canine American cousins, are inclined to extend one hind leg in an "interoceptive reflex" reaction to distention of the bladder. A hygienic synkinesia of this nature is indeed more understandable in any geographic setting than is any association between bladder distention and say, salivation.

3. Visceral states can influence skeletal motor responses, which then in turn modify their visceral concomitants. Moreover, the extent and duration of these resonating "psychosomatic" feedbacks may vary with the temperament and current status of each animal. One is again reminded of George Bernard Shaw's query on reading Pavlov's *Conditioned Reflexes:* "But doesn't every observant dog owner know all this?"

4. Exhaustive stimulation of any portion of the nervous system (e.g., one tibial nerve) can induce other portions (e.g., the other tibialis, or afferent neurons from the gut) to become excessively responsive to stimulation. This displaced neural hyperreactivity penultimate to total exhaustion is also a well-known phenomenon, although why this compensatory alerting should be called *hysteriosis* in an exceedingly strained analogy to neurotic hysteria must be regarded as another well-guarded Russian secret.

5. An urgency to urinate in human beings, as well as in dogs, is influenceable by many social contingencies, among

them, previous numerical associations such as may be con-
notated by the command: "Take a number from 0 to 5."

6. Our Soviet colleagues believe, as we do, that the cortex
has much to do with the coupling and gearing ("dynamic
stereotype"), cross-indexing ("analysis") and redelivery
("directed synthesis") of behavioral patterns.

7. But, they continue, when these cortical functions of
spatiotemporal discrimination and adaptive response are
stressed beyond the organism's integrative capacities, a
"neurotic breakdown" may occur, e.g., as in the Russian
tongue-out-of-cheek and lamp-licking experiments kindly re-
layed to us in appropriate reflexologic dialect. Pavlov would
have approved Dr. Worden's faithful formulation of such
phenomena in terms of "cortical excitation and inhibition,"
but if I read Frolov's [5] intimate accounts of Pavlov's semantic
prejudices correctly, he would have fined any rash disciple
at least 40 groschen for imputing motivation or affect to any
organism, as is implied in Dr. Worden's aside that it seems
unlikely "that the dog cared which side of his tongue was
stimulated first."

All in all, we can be grateful for Dr. Worden's illuminating
review of recent Russian concordances. Indeed, without dis-
tracting from Pavlov's stimulating though somewhat mono-
thetic leadership or the ingenuity and industry of his
followers, we can assure our Russian colleagues that none of
their experimental findings would sound unacceptable (or
particularly novel) to any well-trained American neuro-
physiologist, particularly those familiar with the work of
Ranson, Gantt, Magoun, Delgado, Olds, Lilly, and many
others. Certainly my associates and I, in several score of
research reports in this field, have repeatedly stressed the
multiplicity of genetic, neurophysiologic, symbolic-experien-
tial, social, and other complex transactional vectors that

[5] Frolov, Y. P. *Pavlov and His School*. New York: Oxford University
Press, 1937.

interpenetrate all behavior, whether animal or human, normal or neurotic. We are, then, delighted that our Soviet counterparts are now taking a similarly broad view not only of life in the laboratory but of human conduct in general.

We welcome also Dr. Worden's own modern reorientations with regard to the topological and resonant-inductive rather than topographic-hierarchic nature of CNS organization and his recognition of the essential role of the "ascending reticular system"—which, parenthetically, as an integrative core also "descends," is not altogether "reticular," and makes possible an interplay of many neurophysiologic cadences rather than itself constituting a separable "system." We are not quite as enthused as is Dr. Worden, however, about the brilliant promise of various methods for electrifying the interior of the CNS, whether or not such techniques afford the animal the choice of differential self-stimulation or concomitant external experience. Indeed, after utilizing and developing Ranson's and Magoun's original adaptations of the Horsley-Clarke stereotactic methods for a decade, my associates and I relinquished further studies involving buried electrical or chemical stimulation of the CNS in the early 1940s, because we could never be quite sure of their *experiential* meaning to the animal. (The reasons why are stated in some detail in my book *Behavior and Neurosis,* published in 1943.) To cite a not altogether irrelevant human parallel, we may remember observing people pulling the lever of a vending machine to get a bar of candy, or even merely for the "pleasure" of seeing how much galvanic current they could stand without flinching. The phenomena observed were undoubtedly significant, but they hardly constituted a royal road to an elucidation of all human nature. Nevertheless, in the past five years we have begun to combine experiments involving intracerebral microwave induction in epidermally intact and completely free animals with observations of their spontaneous and learned behavior, in attempts once again to explore the significance of such artificially localized CNS excitation in total adaptation. We are, therefore, in accord with the rationale of Dr. Worden's group in being interested in such studies—provided always that they are placed in their biodynamic context.

The inferences drawn by Dr. Worden from his own work, as he briefly reports it in the latter part of his paper, appear to be sound: namely, that the intensity of the electrophysiologic responses of a cat's brain to a repeated but indifferent auditory stimulus are in some degree correlated with its general behavior. Consequently, such responses can indeed be intensified if the stimulus is made of greater significance to the animal by being paired with a shock to the paw or a high treble note staccatoed in rock-and-roll rhythm, or conversely, they can be decreased if the animal is distracted by other interests. Dr Worden does not specify how he tapped the cochlear nucleus, the trapezoid body, and the auditory cortex of his cats for EEG leads, but I infer it was also by stereotactic electrode implantation. Nor, perhaps for want of time, does he present in detail his experimental protocols, but I again presume that the tracings analyzed in Fig. 2–6 were responses to the signal tone in a mother cat, first during an anesthetized state, then when awake, and finally during successive stages of training. If so, the relative constancy and synchronicity of the multilead tracings, rather than their variability, is the more remarkable phenomenon— and may indicate, contrary to the initial postulate, that the EEG is in such instances a quite deficient index of consciousness, integration, memory, or other truly meaningful CNS activity. Where large waves appear, as in Fig. 2–8, they may be, as Dr. Worden parenthetically notes, coincident with sniffing or lever-pressing and might therefore constitute a resonance of pyramidal or other motor circuits, as is especially marked in Fig. 2–9.

Finally, as a bit of a violinist and a sailor, I am in complete accord with Dr. Worden in his insistence that it helps a great deal to know the structure, function, and optimal adjustment of one's instrument before one essays to play a sonata or embark on a voyage of exploration. And, as Dr. Worden implies, neuropsychiatry—until recently a term of yearning but now rapidly acquiring a new substance and dignity—can, like music and sailing, be all the more satisfying when its functional, pragmatic, and esthetic aspects are exquisitely blended.

References

1. AYRAPET 'YANTS, E. SH. Toward a characterization of interoceptive influences. Article 29, Vol. 1 (reference 51).
2. AYRAPET 'YANTS, E. SH. New materials on interoceptive signaling. Article 29, Vol. 1 (reference 51).
3. AYRAPET 'YANTS, E. SH. New materials on the interconnection of the activity of internal and external analyzers. Article 29, Vol. 1 (reference 51).
4. AYRAPET 'YANTS, E. SH. Interoception and hysteriosis, Article 29, Vol. 1 (reference 51).
5. AYRAPET 'YANTS, E. SH. An attempt at investigating the internal analyzer in man. Article 29, Vol. 1 (reference 51).
6. AYRAPET 'YANTS, E. SH. On I. P. Pavlov's theory in internal analyzers. Article 29, Vol. 1 (reference 51).
7. BICKFORD, P. G., H. W. DODGE, and A. VIHLEIN. Electrographic and behavioral effects related to depth stimulation in the human. *Conference on Electrical Studies in the Unanesthetized Brain, June 10–13, 1957.* Georgetown University Medical School (to be published).
8. DELAFRESHAYE, J. F. *Brain Mechanisms and Consciousness.* Oxford: Blackwell Sci. Publ., 1954.
9. BRAZIER, M. A. B., R. KJELLBERG, W. H. SWEET, and J. S. BARLOW. Electrographic recording with correlation analysis from deep structures within the human brain. *Conference on Electrical Studies on the Unanesthetized Brain, June 10–13, 1957.* Georgetown University Medical School (to be published).
10. BYKOV, K. M., V. M. VASYUTOCHKIN. The biochemical substrate of neural trophicity. Article 15, Vol. 1 (reference 51). *Fiziologichesky Zhurnal SSSR 15:* 555–565 (1954).
11. BYKOV, K. M. Further development of the problem of the physiology and pathology of corticovisceral relationships. Article 30, Vol. 2 (reference 51). *Zhurnal Vysshey Nervnoy Deyatel,* nosti (*J. higher nerv. Activity*), 5: 449–462 (1955).

12. RAMÓN Y CAJAL, S. *Histologie du systeme nerveux de l'homme et les vertèbres.* 2 vols., pp. 948–959. Paris: Maloine, 1909–1911.
13. CHOYNOWSKI, M. Toward egress from stagnation in Polish psychology (in Polish) *Kultura i Spoleczen stwo 1:* 64–83 (1957); cited by Josef Brozek in Physiological psychology. *Amer. Rev. Psychol. 9:* 71–98 (1958).
14. DELGADO, J. M. R., and H. HAMLIN. Spontaneous and evoked electrical seizures in animals and humans. *Conference on Electrical Studies in the Unanesthetized Brain, June 10–13, 1957.* Georgetown University Medical School (to be published).
15. FRENCH, J. D., F. K. AMERONGEN, and H. W. MAGOUN. An activating system in brain stem of monkey. *Arch. Neurol. Psychiat. 68:* 577–590 (1952).
16. FUSTER, JOAQUIN M. Effects of stimulation of brain stem on tachistoscopic perception in monkeys. *Science 127:* 150 (1958).
17. GALAMBOS, R., G. SHEATZ, and V. VERNIER. Electrophysiologic correlates of a conditioned response in cats. *Science 123:* 376–377 (1956).
17a. GANTT, W. A. H. *Physiological Bases of Psychiatry.* Springfield: Charles C Thomas, Publishers, 1958.
18. HEATH, R. G., *et al. Studies in Schizophrenia: A Multidisciplinary Approach to Mind-Brain Relationships,* Robert G. Heath, Chairman. Cambridge, Mass.: Harvard University Press, 1954.
19. HEATH, R. G. Correlations between levels of psychological awareness and physiological activity in the central nervous system. *Psychosomat. Med. 17:* 383–395 (1955).
20. HEBB, D. O. *The Organization of Behaviour.* New York: John Wiley & Sons, Inc., 1949.
21. HERNANDEZ-PEON, R. Central mechanisms controlling conduction along central sensory pathways. *Acta Neurol. Latinoamer. 1:* 256–264 (1955).
22. HERNANDEZ-PEON, R., and K. E. HAGBARTH. Interaction between afferent and cortically induced reticular responses. *J. Neurophysiol. 18:* 44–55 (1955).
23. HERNANDEZ-PEON, R., and H. SCHERRER. "Habituation" to acoustic stimuli in cochlear nucleus. *Federation Proc. 14:* 71 (1955).
24. HERNANDEZ-PEON, R., H. SCHERRER, and M. JOUVET. Modification of electric activity in cochlear nucleus during "attention" in unanesthetized cats. *Science 123:* 331–332 (1956).
25. KAADA, B. R. Somato-motor, autonomic, and electrocorticographic responses to electrical stimulation of "rhinencephalic" and other structures in primates, cat, and dog. *Acta Physiol. Scand. 24,* Suppl. 83 (1951).
26. KLUVER, H., and P. C. BUCY. Preliminary analysis of functions of the temporal lobes in monkeys. *Arch. Neurol. Psychiat. 42:* 979–1000 (1939).
27. KRUSE, H. D. (ed.). *Integrating the Approaches to Mental Illness.* New York: Paul B. Hoeber, Inc., 1958.
28. KUPALOV, P. S. Physiological organization of the processes of excitation and inhibition in the cerebral cortex during conditioned reflex

activity. Article 24, Vol. 1 (reference 51). *Zhurnal vysskey nervnoy deyatel 'norti J. higher vern. Activity 5:* 463–473 (1955).

29. LASHLEY, K. S. In Search of the Engram. In *Physiological Mechanisms in Animal Behaviour.* New York: Academic Press, Inc., 1950.

30. LASHLEY, K. S. Functional interpretation of anatomic patterns. *Res. Publ. Assn. Res. Nerv. Ment. Dis. 30:* 529–547 (1952).

31. LESSE, H., R. G. HEATH, W. A. MICKLE, R. R. MONROE, and W. H. MILLER. Rhinencephalic activity during thought. *J. nerv. ment. Dis. 122:* 433–440 (1955).

31a. LILLY, J. C. Mental effects of reduction of ordinary levels of physical stimuli on intact, healthy patients. In *Psychotherapy with Schizophrenics.* (Eds. E. B. Brody and F. C. Redlich). Pp. 168–178. New York: International Universities Press, Inc., 1952.

32. LINDSLEY, D. B. Higher functions of the central nervous system. *Ann. Rev. Physiol. 17:* 311–338 (1955).

33. LINDSLEY, D. B. The reticular activating system and perceptual integrations. Chap. in Sheer, Daniel E. (ed.). *Electrical Stimulation of the Brain* (Houston Symposium on Brain Stimulation). Austin, Texas: University of Texas Press, 1957.

34. LINDSLEY, D. B., J. BOWDEN, and H. W. MAGOUN. Behavioral and EEG changes following chronic brain stem lesions in the cat. *EEG Clin. Neurophysiol. 1:* 475–486 (1949).

35. LIVINGSTON, R. B., and F. G. WORDEN. Neurophysiology of the Reticular Systems. In press: Sheer, Daniel E. (ed.). *Electrical Stimulation of the Brain* (Houston Symposium on Brain Stimulation). Austin, Texas: University of Texas Press, 1957.

36. LIVINGSTON, R. B., and F. G. WORDEN. Some neurophysiological contributions to internal medicine. *Stanford Med. Bull. 13:* 194–203 (1955).

37. LIVINGSTON, W. K., F. P. HAUGEN, and J. M. BROOKHART. Functional organization of the central nervous system. *Neurology 4:* 485–496 (1954).

38. MACLEAN, P. D. Psychosomatic disease and the "Visceral Brain"; Recent developments bearing on the Papez theory of emotion. *Psychosom. Med. 11:* 338–353 (1949).

39. MAGOUN, H. W. The ascending reticular activating system. *Res. Publ. Assn. nerv. ment. Dis. 30:* 480–492 (1952).

40. MENNINGER, K., H. ELLENBERGER, P. PRUYSER, and M. MAYMAN. The unitary concept of mental illness. *Bull. Menninger Clinic 22:* 4–12 (1958).

41. MORUZZI, G., and H. W. MAGOUN. Brain stem reticular formation and activation of the EEG. *EEG Clin. Neurophysiol. 1:* 455–473 (1949).

42. OLDS, J. Self-stimulation of the brain. *Science 127:* 315–324 (1958).

43. OLDS, J., and P. MILNER. Positive reinforcement produced by electrical stimulation of septal area and other regions of rat brain. *J. comp. Physiol. Psychol. 47:* 419–427 (1954).

44. OSTOW, M. A psychoanalytic contribution to the study of brain function, Part II & III. *Psychoanal. Quart. 24:* 383–423 (1955).

45. PAPEZ, J. A proposed mechanism of emotion. *Arch. Neurol. Psychiat. 38:* 725–743 (1937).

46. PRIBRAM, K. H., and L. KRUGER. Functions of the "olfactory brain."
    Ann. N. Y. Acad. Sci. 58: 109–138 (1954).
46a. RANSON, S. W. *Anatomy of the Nervous System, Its Development and
    Function.* 9th ed. Rev. by S. L. Clark. Philadelphia: W. B. Saunders
    Company, 1953.
47. RAZRAN, GREGORY. Soviet psychology since 1950. *Science 126:* 1100–
    1107 (1957).
48. SAWA, M., Y. UEKI, M. ARITA, and T. HARADA. Preliminary report on
    the amygdaloidectomy on the psychotic patients, with interpretation
    of oral-emotional manifestation in schizophrenia. *Folio Psychiat.
    Neurol. (Japan) 4:* 309–329 (1954).
49. SCHEIBEL, M., and A. SCHEIBEL. Structural substrates for integrative
    patterns in the brain stem reticular core. In: *Reticular Formation of
    the Brain.* Boston: Little, Brown & Company, 1958.
50. SCHEIBEL, M., A. SCHEIBEL, A. MOLLICA, and G. MORUZZI. Conver-
    gence and interaction of afferent impulses on single units of reticular
    formation. *J. Neurophysiol. 18:* 309–331 (1955).
51. *Selected Articles in the Central Nervous System and Behavior.* 2
    vols. English translations of 75 Russian and 4 Scandinavian articles
    prepared by the National Medical Library as background material
    for the First Conference on Central Nervous System and Behavior,
    Josiah Macy, Jr. Foundation Conference Program.
52. SPERRY, R. W. On the neural basis of the conditioned response. *Brit.
    J. Animal Behav. 3:* 41–44 (1955).
53. TERZIAN, H., and G. DALLE ORE. Syndrome of Klüver and Bucy re-
    produced in man by bilateral removal of the temporal lobes. *Neu-
    rology 5:* 373–380 (1955).
54. TEUBER, HANS-LUKAS. Physiological psychology. *Amer. Rev. Psychol.
    6:* 267–296 (1955). See especially pp. 270–275.

3

Recent Biochemical Investigations in Schizophrenia

C. H. HARDIN BRANCH [1] AND JOY W. ELY [2]

The investigations into the physiological and biochemical phenomena accompanying schizophrenia have in the past been of two major types. We may borrow from the literature of fairy stories and call one the *Rumpelstiltskin school of thought* which holds that if something can be labeled it can be understood. The other we may call the *Titwillow school* after the tomtit in *The Mikado* whose depression was said to be due to "weakness of intellect" or "an extra tough worm" or "blighted affection." This school would maintain that mental illness must be due *either* to basic hereditary factors, *or* to metabolic changes in the individual, *or* to some difficulty in object relationships.

Unfortunately neither of these approaches has been very effective. Multidisciplinary research—perhaps this could be called the *Little Red Hen school*—is today in the ascendancy and may offer a better approach to the problem. One cannot avoid the irreverent comment that integrated endeavor or "togetherness" is prominent in all aspects of American life

[1] Professor and Head, Department of Psychiatry, College of Medicine, University of Utah, Salt Lake City.
[2] Teaching Assistant, Department of Psychiatry, College of Medicine, University of Utah, Salt Lake City.

from the Armed Forces to the popular magazines, yet this movement will at least avoid some of the pitfalls inherent in the other two schools of thought.

Advocates of the multidisciplinary method should have all-track minds and perform on all-star teams. The trick is to be able to think simultaneously along several lines about the same subject. The improvements in communication should be of considerable value, and meanwhile, the facts that the psychiatrist often does not understand what the biochemist is talking about, and vice versa, and that there is no demonstrable connection between the oedipal complex and the glyoxylic acid test for urinary indoles are not too important.

This multifaceted, multidimensional approach to the problem of schizophrenia probably will be productive. At least it is *sensible,* because it forces us to think of multiple concurrent etiologic factors rather than of a final single cause. Psychiatrists have not always been famous for ability to do this. Their preoccupation with "ultimate cause" attests their kinship to philosophers and theologians rather than to other medical scientists. Hoffer (1) implies that the true scientist should be more concerned with the how than with the why of things, and goes on to say, "In medicine, we do not treat causes—we treat those variables most easily modified, and these may be physiological, psychological, electrical, or combinations of these." Diabetes mellitus is a good example of an extremely complex metabolic disease in which accumulation of the what-and-how type of knowledge has led to a lifesaving form of treatment, even though the actual cause of the condition is unknown. If we never do more than clarify concurrent functional pathways and meaningfully relate them to each other, we shall have come a long way with the intricate and fascinating problem of schizophrenia.

Caution is necessary in evaluating interdisciplinary studies for several reasons. Both the psychological and the biochemical variables must be carefully defined. It should be obvious that questionable behavioral criteria cannot be accepted, nor can undue credence be given to biochemical determinations which are not reproducible or which have dubious interpretative significance.

Both biological and psychological techniques present difficult problems in quantification, and Horwitt (2) has stated that many reports showing differences between schizophrenic and "normal" individuals are based on environmental artifacts not related to the basic disorder. He lists the intervening variables of emotional stress, tension and anxiety, nutritional state, liver function, athletic training, and diurnal variation in activity as factors which must be controlled.

The question of whether schizophrenia is a single disease entity or a group of symptomatically similar, but basically unrelated, disorders cannot be ignored. A tenable, although unproved, assumption seems to be that there is at least *one* true disease entity, *process schizophrenia,* among the schizophrenias, but that there are many *schizophrenoform* reactions of varying etiology. This is not surprising in view of the fact that the reaction patterns of the human organism must of necessity be limited. Consequently, since the number of symptoms we can develop is not infinite, we can expect that a host of apparently unrelated conditions may result in the production of symptoms which will resemble each other— a sort of symptomatic "final common pathway."

In essence, the present conceptualization of schizophrenia is not unlike that of "consumption" many years ago. In both situations the initial concern was with dramatic common symptoms which appeared in several conditions. It was many years before the consumptions were separated into distinct entities with various etiologies, and we are only now beginning this process with the schizophrenias. In addition, we have the problem that some diagnoses of schizophrenia are made on a social value system, and simply mean *different* or *unwanted.* In a culture where gregariousness, other-directedness, and good communication are valued, the qualities of seclusiveness and withdrawal from relationships will seem out of joint. Even in his own home, the person who sits quietly without doing anything will invariably be asked, "What's the matter? Are you sick?" Sometimes it seems that society is asking this same question when it labels as schizophrenic the person who lacks ambition or has a unique system of values.

Biological investigations of schizophrenia have been steadily increasing since the turn of the century.

It is curious to note that Berger in 1904 found and reported a toxin in the blood of catatonic patients which had an exciting effect on the cortical motor center of dogs. Endocrine function, carbohydrate and oxygen metabolism, temperature regulation, and circulatory mechanisms were among the many aspects of schizophrenic physiology investigated by earlier workers. The over-all biological picture of the schizophrenic which emerged from these earlier studies was described by Hoskins (3) in 1946 as being marked by a general deficiency in adaptive efficiency or ability to maintain homeostasis.

The lack of robustness of personality and physiology in the schizophrenic has an interesting corollary in Kallmann's observations (4). Kallmann feels that the schizophrenic has a lack of *genetic* robustness which expresses itself in a more general deficiency of resistance.

It may well be that there is a genetically nonspecific constitutional weakness in those factors which contribute to an adequate defense system, and the high tuberculosis morbidity and fatality rates in schizophrenics may be part of this general picture. Further, if one of monozygotic twins develops schizophrenia, the twin who is "strong" enough to escape schizophrenia will also have shown a consistent developmental picture from early childhood of superior physical strength and body weight. This physical difference does not appear in monozygotic twins who are concordant as to schizophrenia. The frequent observation of asthenic body types in schizophrenics may be related to this concept of generally impaired resistance.

Kallmann's finding of the very impressive expectancy rate for schizophrenia, when consanguinity is taken into account (86 per cent of monozygotic twins, as compared to 14 per cent in full siblings and dizygotic twins) is, of course, well known. These genetic studies were first published in 1938 but did not receive the attention they deserved until the last few years. They seem to offer strong evidence against any theory of exclusively environmental—or psychogenic, in the sense of dualism between mind and body—etiology. Further investigations of identical twins reared apart will help to clarify the modifying impact of environment on heredity.

In very recent years there has been an intensification of interest in the biochemical aspects of schizophrenia, brought about by the advent of the psychotomimetic and tranquilizing drugs. In spite of the increasingly great amount of work being reported in this field, however, there is as yet no definitely substantiated, incontrovertible evidence of specific biochemical aberration in schizophrenia other than the genetic studies. Nor do we find any reason to believe that a single etiologic factor for the "disease" will be demonstrated. Rather, a reasonable hypothesis might be that a predisposing genetic factor is transmitted in the form of aberrant enzyme metabolism, and the degree of expression of the metabolic defect is determined by influences ranging from the molecular to the social-behavioral level.

Before summarizing recent biochemical investigations in schizophrenia, two final points must be made: (1) This paper is not an attempt at a complete survey but only an effort to give an over-all highlighted view of the biochemical scene. Mention of many specific pieces of work has been omitted because of limitations of space and time. (2) In spite of the incompleteness of our present-day biochemical understanding of schizophrenia, there is every indication that work in this area holds great promise. One cannot fail to be intrigued by the relationships and interlocking phenomena which have already emerged and which suggest that the gestalt is there.

SEROTONIN

Many of the known hallucinogenic and tranquilizing drugs, and in addition the endogenous substance serotonin, which probably plays a role in brain function, have certain biochemical structural characteristics in common. This observation may or may not be significant; it is certainly provocative and it is the starting point of much of the research that has been done in recent years.

Epinephrine has been implicated in central-nervous-system function since Cannon's observations (5) in 1929 on its relation to emotion and stress. Weil-Malherbe (6) has recently described a broad correlation between the plasma epinephrine level and the level of consciousness or extent of nervous activity; and Funkenstein (7) has attempted to link the ratio of epinephrine: norepinephrine secretion in psychotic patients to their emotional state. Mescaline has an even longer psychiatric history than epinephrine, for it was known, at least as early as the turn of the century, to be capable of producing psychotic symptoms. The first systematic attempt to relate the two compounds to schizophrenia did not occur, however, until the publication in 1952 of Osmond and Smythies' paper, "Schizophrenia: A New Approach" (8). These workers commented on the structural similarity of epinephrine and mescaline and hypothesized that schizophrenia might be due to a specific metabolic disorder in which abnormal breakdown of epinephrine resulted in the accumulation of a toxic substance similar to mescaline.

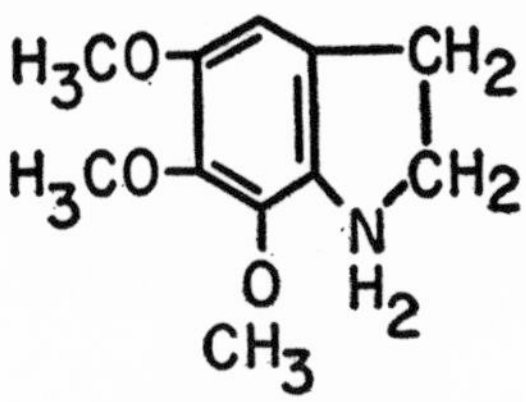

MESCALINE

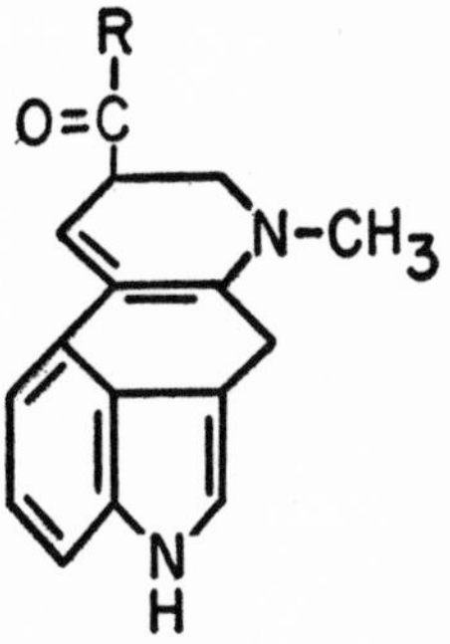

LSD

In the following year, Hoffer, Osmond, and Smythies (9) reported preliminary experiments with hallucinogens and gave special attention to the action of adrenochrom, an oxidation product of epinephrine which, unlike epinephrine, has an indole nucleus.

In 1952 Rinkel *et al.* (10, 11) did a related type of work with lysergic acid diethylamide (LSD), noting the psychologic and autonomic changes following its administration. They postulated that LSD interfered with a major enzyme system and felt that clinical responses implicated the epinephrine cycle. They were unable to reproduce the psychotomimetic action of adrenochrom noted by Hoffer, Osmond, and Smythies, but felt that adrenoxine, a further oxidation product of epinephrine whose chemical structure is unknown, might be hallucinogenic. In their most recent paper, Hoffer and Osmond (12) suggest that schizophrenia is an autonomic disease produced by an increase in concentration and activity of acetylcholine centrally and abnormal diversion of epinephrine into a toxic indole. Any compound which blocks acetylcholinesterase, causing an increased production of epinephrine, and which is converted to an indole or is itself an indole, might be implicated. Pope *et al.* (13) have found the acetylcholinesterase activity of frontal cortex specimens to be variable but generally higher in psychotic than in nonpsychotic subjects. It is emphasized that a higher rate of acetylcholine metabolism is only inferred, not proved, by the finding of higher acetylcholinesterase activity; that the finding is more likely to be the result of long-standing mental illness than of significance in its etiology; and that the number of determinations is small.

Our own work with LSD-25 seems to indicate that its effect is largely a nonspecific toxic one, but the fact that the effect is considerably more marked following 24–48 hours of induced wakefulness has led us to check the sleep patterns of patients prior to their acute schizophrenic episodes. A surprising number showed considerable sleep disturbance preceding the psychosis. Confirmation of this impression could lead to the practical suggestion that management of the insomnia might have aborted the attack.

As we have already seen, observation of the structural similarity of some hallucinogenic and some tranquilizing drugs led to the hypothesis that if a naturally occurring hallucinogen existed, it would also belong to this broad class of activated aromatic compounds. McGeer *et al.* (14) tested this by determining the urinary excretory pattern of aromatic compounds in schizophrenics and "normals" and confirmed the previous work of others by reporting more diazo-coupling compounds in the urine of schizophrenics than in the urine of "normals" or patients with other mental disorders. Riegelhaupt (15) reported positive urinary glyoxylic acid reactions in the majority of schizophrenics and negative reactions in the majority of nonschizophrenics. It is pre-

sumed that the schizophrenics excrete in the urine a substance with an indole nucleus, possibly a tryptophan metabo-
lite.

We are presently investigating the finding that an indole
(as yet unidentified) appears in the urines of 60 per cent of
schizophrenic patients as compared to 15 per cent of "normals." These ratios have held up over a period of two years
and do not seem to be affected by hospitalization, diet,
chronicity of the illness, or the type of treatment given.
There is a suggestion—no more—that a positive indole finding
may correlate with certain specific psychologic data in both
patients and controls, regardless of the diagnosis.

Since it is known that the precursors of most of the activated aromatic compounds in the body are the dietary amino
acids, McGeer et al. (16) hypothesized that a diet lacking
in these elements would alter the abnormal excretory pattern
of schizophrenics. This proved to be the case; the patterns
showed a reduction to normal or near-normal levels. Oddly
enough, Bogoch (17) found that a diet grossly deficient in
aromatic amino acids was associated with definite clinical
deterioration in more than half of a test group of schizophrenics. Cafruny and Domino (18) have reported a deficient urinary concentration of a hydroxylated indole or
tryptophan derivative in schizophrenics, but they feel that,
even though previous studies indicate excessive concentra-
tions of certain aromatic constituents, it is quite possible that
a concomitant deficiency in other constituents may exist.

In 1956 Heath and his coworkers began a series of studies
which have led to interesting findings. The level of reduced
glutathione had been previously noted by Altschule et al.
(19) to be lower in the blood of psychotic than in that of
normal subjects. This finding was confirmed by Heath's
group (20, 21, 22). They noted also that the copper-carrying
enzyme, ceruloplasmin, is an in vitro oxidizer of both glutathione and epinephrine. Remembering Osmond's and

Rinkel's speculation that faulty epinephrine metabolism might be the cause of schizophrenic symptoms (and combining this with their own theory that schizophrenics show abnormal EEG recordings from the septal and hippocampal regions of the brain and that the septal region may have some control over epinephrine metabolism), Heath and his group began experiments on the reactions in vitro between epinephrine and plasma from schizophrenic and nonschizophrenic subjects. They found that schizophrenic plasma produced faster in vitro oxidation of epinephrine and postulated that this phenomenon was due to increased quantities of ceruloplasmin. Because this is a nonspecific reaction and is encountered also with plasma from patients with chronic infections, terminal malignancies, and in convalescence from acute infections, Heath hypothesized that there might be a qualitative difference between the copper-containing enzyme of schizophrenics and persons without psychotic behavior. Akerfeldt (23) and Abood et al. (24) confirmed the observation that the plasma of patients with schizophrenia and certain other conditions showed increased oxidation of neurohumoral amines, but they pointed out that the reaction was due not only to increased ceruloplasmin activity but also to decreased ascorbic acid concentration. (Ascorbic acid is a principal reducing agent of serum.) Horwitt (25), on the other hand, found no important differences in the total serum copper (96 per cent of serum copper is normally bound to ceruloplasmin) or in its rate of catecholamine oxidation in schizophrenic and nonschizophrenic sera, and he warned of the necessity for ruling out inflammation, infection, and nutritional deficiency in evaluating these studies. Aprison and Drew (26) have recently confirmed Horwitt's findings, reporting no significant differences between catecholamine oxidation in sera from schizophrenic and nonschizophrenic children.

Subsequent studies of Heath's group (27) seem to agree with Horwitt's observations, showing no significant difference between total serum copper levels of schizophrenics and normal controls, and demonstrating that prior administration of ascorbic acid results in striking decrease in catecholamine oxidation rates of both schizophrenic and normal sera. However, in recent articles: (1) Heath (28) has suggested that there may be some correlation between higher ceruloplasmin levels and higher remission rates in schizophrenics and reports the attempted therapeutic administration of ceruloplasmin. (2) Ostfeld, Abood, and Marcus (29) state that a recently synthesized atropinelike hallucinogen caused increased levels of ceruloplasmin in seven of nine patients, that intravenous infusion of four catecholamines (including epinephrine and serotonin) had no effect on ceruloplasmin level, and that serum ceruloplasmin was significantly higher in a group of neurotic patients exhibiting disturbed behavior than in those who were tranquil. At the conclusion of this rather rambling account of ceruloplasmin, it scarcely needs to be added that its relationship to schizophrenia—if any— needs further clarification.

In 1957 the attention of Heath et al. (30) became diverted from their studies of ceruloplasmin to a related compound which they feel is of great importance in schizophrenia. In the process of isolating the ceruloplasmin fraction from schizophrenic and normal serum, these workers noted that the euglobulin precipitate from schizophrenics had a blue color, whereas that from "normals" did not. They developed a technique for processing this substance and named it taraxein. They first administered taraxein to monkeys and noted that it caused behavioral changes which they felt were remarkably similar to those of schizophrenia; encephalographic recordings from electrodes implanted in the septal and hippocampal regions showed the alterations which this group believes to be characteristic of schizophrenia. Taraxein has now been given to seventeen nonpsychotic and three schizophrenic (in remission) human volunteers. In all these individuals, symptoms appeared which were interpreted as schizophreniclike; these did not appear in subjects receiving ostensibly the same protein fraction isolated from normal serum or other control substances. On the assumption that unprocessed schizophrenic plasma must contain a precursor of taraxein, they injected the plasma intravenously into four subjects and reported transient behavioral changes which did not occur in two subjects receiving nonschizophrenic plasma. There have been some difficulties in reproducing this work in other laboratories, but some confirmatory reports have appeared and it should be noted that the extraction technique itself is difficult.

The immediate question which arises about this work is that of the clinical diagnostic criteria for schizophrenia. Certainly, most of us would agree with Bleuler (32) that disturbance of the associative processes is the pathognomonic symptom of schizophrenia, but the statement in Heath's reports that the overwhelming majority of people seeking outpatient psychiatric therapy are schizophrenic, indicates that the diagnostic criteria in these cases are different or are applied differently from what is ordinarily the case. It is of interest, however, that taraxein is said not to produce the visual hallucinations and autonomic changes characteristic of LSD administration. Certainly, we shall all be watching further developments of this work with great interest, and it is of prime necessity that other groups attempt to reproduce it.

To return now to the saga of the indole nucleus, we find it making a fascinating reappearance in the form of serotonin. Serotonin had been known for some time to be a potent constrictor of smooth muscle. Psychiatrically significant discoveries about this compound were not made until 1953, when it was found to be a naturally occurring constituent of animal brain tissue, and its muscle-constricting action was shown to be antagonized by minute quantities of LSD. Woolley and Shaw (33) were the first to develop the concept that serotonin might have a function in maintaining normal mental processes and that changes in its concentration (either increase or decrease) in the brain could lead to mental and neurological disorder. They have subsequently demonstrated that serotonin has the same contractile effect on the oligodendroglia cells of animal and human brain that it has on smooth muscle and that this contractile action is overcome by some, but not all, of its structural analogues. Brodie, Pletscher, and Shore (34, 35, 36) have shown by animal studies that the tranquilizing drug, reserpine, liberates both serotonin and norepinephrine from their body depots, peripheral as well as central. Their concept of the mechanism of serotonin release is as follows: Serotonin in the brain is normally present in a bound, inactive form, thus being protected from the highly active enzyme, monamine oxidase. Reserpine impairs the ability of the brain cells to store serotonin and it is liberated in its free form. Since it is rapidly metabolized, the total serotonin content of the brain is lowered, but as long as the storing capacity of the cells remains impaired there is an increase in the amount of free serotonin, which is thought to be the physiologically active form.

Brodie and Shore (37) propose the concept that serotonin is the chemical transmitter of the central parasympathetic system and that norepinephrine is the transmitter of the central sympathetic system. They speculate that a continuous flow of highly active free serotonin in small amounts stimulates the synapses of the central parasympathetic division, and that an excessive concentration has the same effect as a substance which blocks its action. This theory has the advantage of reconciling the seemingly conflicting evidence that either deficiency or excess of serotonin might be therapeutic.

We have seen that Cannon's emergency stress theory of the adrenal medulla first brought epinephrine into psychiatry. Similarly, the well-known *general adaptation syndrome* in relation to stress, described by Hans Selye (37a), suggested that the relationship of adrenocortical and pituitary function to schizophrenia might be a fruitful area for study. This has been the subject of detailed investigation by Hoagland, Pincus, *et al.* (38, 39, 40) over a period of many years. They have used blood eosinophil and lymphocyte levels, and urinary excretion of potassium, sodium, phosphate, "corticoids," uric acid, and 17-ketosteroids as indices of adrenocortical function, and have compared schizophrenics with "normals," both at rest and in response to stress. Although there is some variation in the individual indices, this group feels that the over-all picture which emerges in the schizophrenic is one of relative adrenal hypofunction *in response to stress.* Because of differences in the data obtained from different age groups, it is hypothesized that the major defect in older schizophrenics is at the hypothalamic level of the pituitary, while in younger schizophrenics it is at the level of the adrenal cortex.

Bliss *et al.* (41) measuring the concentration of adrenal steroids in peripheral blood following administration of ACTH and insulin, found no evidence of impaired adrenocortical or pituitary-adrenal function in schizophrenics. These findings, although not in direct opposition to those of the Worcester group because of the different measurements used, point out the need for further study before definite conclusions can be drawn.

Hoagland, Rinkel, and Hyde (42) have attempted to relate steroid metabolism to catecholamine metabolism (that is, the adrenal cortex to the medulla) by comparing the urinary excretion of phosphate in LSD-produced psychosis to that in schizophrenia. In both conditions there is a low resting phosphate excretion, but a gross increase in response to ACTH, not seen in normals. This finding, they feel, suggests that LSD acts on enzyme systems which facilitate the binding of phosphate, and that an endogenous derivative of epinephrine metabolism may have the same action in schizophrenics. They propose that the corticoids release the bound form of phosphate. Finally, Rinkel et al. (43) state that LSD seems to stimulate the pituitary-adrenal system, leaving the adrenal somewhat unresponsive to ACTH as measured by excretion of 17-ketosteroids, sodium, and uric acid, and resulting in a condition similar to that seen in schizophrenics.

This review cannot be concluded without mentioning the extensive investigations of Altschule et al. (44, 45, 46, 47, 48, 49) into the general features of carbohydrate metabolism in mental disease. This group has reported a characteristic picture of disordered intermediary carbohydrate metabolism in psychotic subjects as follows: (1) one-third of the patients show elevated levels of fasting blood glucose and lactic acid; (2) after oral administration of glucose, there is a lag in return to the fasting level of true blood glucose, an excessive elevation in lactic and pyruvic acids, a rise rather than a fall in citric and alpha-ketoglutaric acids, and an increased and prolonged fall in serum inorganic phosphate. Manifestation of most of these abnormalities is more marked in acute than in chronic psychoses; the pattern is not specific, however, and is found in other diseases. Clinical improvement following insulin or electroshock therapy is correlated with biochemical changes toward the normal in all these values, and glutathione administration in large doses was reported to produce complete reversion to normal of the carbohydrate pattern, although no therapeutic effect was noted. These investigators believe the adrenal cortex to be hyperactive in acute psychoses and hypoactive in chronic psychoses; they reported that ACTH and hydrocortisone administered to four chronic patients altered the pattern of disordered carbohydrate metabolism so that it more closely resembled that of acute patients. On the basis of these data, it is theorized that the abnormal carbohydrate metabolism of psychotic patients may be related to abnormal adrenocortical function.

Summary

This review of the present biochemical investigations in schizophrenia is obviously incomplete. It is probable that data derived from these—and other similar—sources may help to clarify both the diagnostic and the therapeutic pictures in schizophrenia. It is highly unlikely that biochemistry, at least in the narrow sense of the word, will provide complete explanations for the multidetermined aberrations in human behavior which together constitute the mental illnesses. But certainly these investigations underline the absolute necessity for the development of complete communication between the experts in psychodynamics and the experts in biochemistry, neurophysiology, and the related sciences.

As a final note, it may be well to add that interdisciplinary research has an effect on the participants which may, in the long run, be as important as the research results themselves. Improvement of communications, the interchange of suggestions as to working models or research approaches—these are tangible and worthwhile goals.

Discussion

Robert G. Heath [3]

Dr. Branch has presented a beautifully organized review of a most complicated subject and, in so doing, has demonstrated a super LRH (little red hen) approach which not

[3] Professor and Chairman, Department of Psychiatry and Neurology, Tulane University School of Medicine, New Orleans.

only covers many divergent areas but also manages to integrate them into an understandable theme.

The author first discusses vicissitudes of methodology in approaching this most difficult problem (one hesitates to use the word *disease* at this juncture). Then, with undue apology, he presents a succinct, yet comprehensive, review of the highlights of the biochemical research program currently under way. Throughout this presentation a theme is developed to the effect that schizophrenia probably is not one disease entity in the usual sense.

In regard to Dr. Branch's comments concerning methodology, we heartily agree that the LRH or multidisciplinary research is necessary. There are some drawbacks to this approach, however: chiefly, the danger of chaos developing as a result of inadequate communication and integration of effort in approaching the common goal. A pecking order is much needed. One or more persons must develop at least a working knowledge of the techniques of all disciplines in the program and, as in all hierarchic arrangements, some individual freedoms must be sacrificed.

Dr. Branch cautions concerning the need for careful evaluation of reports showing differences between normals and schizophrenics. He stresses several factors which need to be considered. But, in addition, there is a very real need for value judgment of the many variables. All too often in present-day research, so much stress is placed on control of inconsequentials that progress is lost in an obsessive morass.

In this context, an addition is offered here to Dr. Branch's remarks concerning so-called nonreproducible results. It is important to know exact techniques and, in addition, all factors involved in an experiment that is to be repeated. This is especially true in regard to the isolation of active biological fractions. Those familiar with the history of the isolation of active fractions of the pituitary will recall that, at best, active fractions could be obtained on only three out of ten occasions, even by the most skilled chemists. This difficulty persisted for a period of over three years until a method finally was evolved whereby very pure fractions could be isolated. In initial experiments, in which fractions were not pure, they often were apt to contain proteolytic components which destroyed the active agent. Not only were there problems in isolating active fractions of the pituitary, but another example is the difficulty Dr. Wendel Stanley encountered in attempting to demonstrate that viruses were made up of nucleoproteins. Sometimes persons attempt a procedure without having thoroughly mastered the technique; they will employ the procedure on a few occasions and then report negative results. This practice is to be deplored for the very practical reason that it often inhibits further research in important areas. It is only fair to stress the fact that a person attempting to repeat an experiment must do so under the exactly same conditions as the original investigators and then only after thoroughly mastering the technique. This is a subject which carries considerable charge for me at the moment, since some difficulties have been encountered in repeating our taraxein studies.

The data which Dr. Branch has reviewed from the literature are presented in a clear and concise manner. The only pertinent additional remarks to be made are to clarify some of the issues regarding the work at Tulane. These remarks will be concerned largely with data which have already been presented at meetings but which are not yet available in published form and, therefore, which Dr. Branch could not review for this presentation.

The Role of Ceruloplasmin. From the published literature, Dr. Branch felt there was some confusion concerning our interpretation of the role of ceruloplasmin. We frequently find ceruloplasmin to be elevated in acute schizophrenic patients but have not found it to be elevated in chronic schizophrenics. We similarly noted that the acute schizophrenics who showed elevated ceruloplasmin levels, in the absence of any general systemic disease, tended to respond more promptly to hospital treatment. It is our thought that an elevated ceruloplasmin may represent a type of nonspecific defense not unlike the increase in white blood count in response to infection. Pursuing this hypothesis, we administered ceruloplasmin to a small group of schizophrenic patients and the acute cases seemingly responded favorably to the administration of large amounts of ceruloplasmin (we doubled their levels). Dr. Sten Martens reported, at the last meeting of the Society of Biological Psychiatry, on a similar therapeutic response in a group of some twenty schizophrenic patients. In his study the acute schizophrenics responded to the intravenous administration of large amounts of ceruloplasmin. Martens also reported that chronic schizophrenic patients who did not respond to the ceruloplasmin per se seemed to become more responsive to electroshock after their ceruloplasmin levels were increased. We, of course, do not believe that the increased ceruloplasmin levels in any way are specific to schizophrenia. In fact, our findings are quite to the contrary.

Taraxein Confirmation. We encountered taraxein while investigating ceruloplasmin in schizophrenic patients. The question of whether or not our findings regarding the psychotoxic substance, taraxein, in schizophrenics can be confirmed has been discussed recently at several meetings. Five research groups have conscientiously attempted to confirm our taraxein findings. There may be others. Four of the five groups have reported that they have been successful. The most widely publicized study, however, was that of the St. Louis group who were unable to confirm our findings. It is only fair to point out that they processed their serum under considerably different circumstances, the principal variation being a significant difference in the pH of the water used for dialysis. The Swedish group (Melander, Martens, *et al.*)

have a confirmatory paper currently in press. Other groups who have demonstrated a psychotoxic factor specific in schizophrenic serum are the Upjohn Company, Dr. John Griffith at the University of Tennessee, and the Merck, Sharp & Dohme Laboratories (Dr. Charles Winters).

The Nature of the Symptoms Resulting from Taraxein. Dr. Branch has noted in his paper that we have not presented in extensive detail the symptoms which we have been able to induce in our volunteer subjects by administering taraxein. This is indeed true, and this shortcoming in our published articles is due to the fact that at all meetings we have demonstrated our findings with films which we believe are a more effective medium for presenting such data.

Current Studies with Taraxein. At present we are investigating the interrelationship between the psychotoxic blood fraction, taraxein, and the altered brain activity which it induces (i.e., the altered brain physiology demonstrated to be consistently present in association with schizophrenic behavior).

If one were to form a gestalt, based on current data from many laboratories, concerning the nature of the underlying biochemical aberrations in schizophrenia, it would be logical to conclude that schizophrenia seems to be associated with some sort of aberration in the area of amine metabolism.

Dr. Branch's remarks concerning the nature of schizophrenia are especially interesting, in particular, that he does not consider it to be one disease entity but rather a sort of symptomatic "final common pathway." This concept is based largely on clinical data; more specifically, the variability in presenting symptoms and the clinical course. Also, the positive evidence for a single common denominator in the form of a biological aberration is as yet quite slim. This, of course, can be interpreted in two ways: (1) schizophrenia is not a single disease entity, as advanced by Dr. Branch; (2) the evidence merely indicates that the fundamental basic biological mechanism has not been demonstrated conclusively as yet, and the differences in symptomatology presented by different patients labeled as schizophrenic are a result of individual characteristics rather than differences in the basic process—the interpretation favored by me. Further to this point, we should be sufficiently flexible to allow for the possibility that with the demonstration of a common, basic biological factor in schizophrenia, there may be even a wider variability in the nature of presenting clinical symptoms. This would imply that there is a possibility that schizophrenia is even more widespread than considered currently by most clinicians. Reference to a common, basic biological factor does not imply that this is the only etiological factor. Certainly, multiple etiologies are associated with every disease. In tuberculosis, fatigue, emotional tensions, malnutrition, and many other factors can contribute, but the common denominator of a Koch's bacillus must be present for this disease to develop. When I refer to the possibility of there being a basic biological factor in schizophrenia, I am referring to something that would be analogous to the Koch's bacillus in tuberculosis. Naturally other etiological factors also would be involved. There is, however, a need for a value judgment of the various etiological factors. In the case of schizophrenia, we know from everyday clinical experience that emotional stress is a very important factor. Probably chemical factors associated with stress will be implicated in the fundamental biological disorder.

Clearly pointed out by Dr. Branch in his paper and in my discussion is the very nuclear factor that there are many differences between schizophrenic patients. Those who postulate that schizophrenia is a single biological entity must be ever aware of this; our working hypothesis must be a flexible one. This, however, is not an unusual state of affairs since it prevails in regard to other disease processes. We must consider that patients susceptible to diseases have varying degrees of resistance. These often are considered constitutional factors. There is a constant dynamic, fluctuating interrelationship between this factor, commonly referred to as a *resistance of the host,* and the ever-changing environmental influences, whether they be in the form of early or childhood traumata or current precipitating factors.

In our conceptual scheme, we have assumed that the fundamental biological aberration in association with the disease, schizophrenia, is in the broad area of an altered constitutional factor, or resistance of the host, and that this is genetically determined. In our hypothesis this deficit is assumed to be a fundamental biochemical one; more specifically, taraxein is considered to be the genetically determined aberration in schizophrenia. We hypothesize that it acts by inhibiting enzyme activity in the brain—enzymes which act on stress transmitters. Thus, we postulate that there is a fundamental biochemical deficit which operates in the general area of affecting the stress chemistry; as a result of this impairment there is a focal physiological alteration in the brain accounting for psychotic behavior. In this regard, it would appear that Berger's seemingly isolated observation in 1904 may prove to have some foundation in fact. If known transmitters, e.g., the amines, were permitted to accumulate in the brain, they indeed could induce an exciting effect on cortical motor centers, as Berger states. It is our responsibility to demonstrate this mechanism so clearly that it can be repeated by persons working in other laboratories. Until we have fulfilled this responsibility, we cannot take strong issue with Dr. Branch's interpretation of the available data.

References

1. HOFFER, A. Biology of schizophrenia (letter to the editor). *Science* 125: 457 (1957).
2. HORWITT, M. K. Fact and artifact in the biology of schizophrenia. *Science 124:* 429 (1956).

2a. BERGER, H. Experimentelle studien zur pathogenese der geistes-krankheiten. *Monatschr. f. Psychiat. u. Neurol. 26,* 1: 213 (1904).

3. HOSKINS, R. G. *The Biology of Schizophrenia.* New York: W. W. Norton & Company, Inc., 1946.

4. KALLMANN, F. J. *Heredity in Health and Mental Disorder.* New York: W. W. Norton & Company, Inc., 1953.

5. CANNON, W. B. *Bodily Changes in Pain, Hunger, Fear and Rage.* Boston: Charles T. Branford Company, 1929.

6. WEIL-MALHERBE, H. The concentration of adrenalin in human plasma and its relation to mental activity. *J. ment. Sci. 101:* 733 (1955).

7. FUNKENSTEIN, D. H. Nor-epinephrine-like and epinephrine-like sub-stances in relation to human behavior. *J. nerv. ment. Dis. 124:* 58 (1956).

8. OSMOND, H., and M. B. SMYTHIES. Schizophrenia: A new approach. *J. ment. Sci. 98:* 309 (1952).

9. HOFFER, A., H. OSMOND, and J. SMYTHIES. Schizophrenia: A new ap-proach II. *J. ment. Sci. 100:* 29 (1954).

10. RINKEL, M., H. J. DESHON, R. W. HYDE, and H. C. SOLOMON. Experi-mental schizophrenia-like symptoms. *Amer. J. Psychiat. 108:* 572 (1952).

11. RINKEL, M., R. W. HYDE, and H. D. SOLOMON. Experimental psychi-atry I: A chemical concept of psychosis. *Dis. nerv. System 15:* 259 (1954).

12. HOFFER, A., and H. OSMOND. Schizophrenia—an autonomic disease. *J. nerv. ment. Dis. 122:* 448 (1955).

13. POPE, A., W. CAVENESS, and K. E. LIVINGSTON. Architectonic distribu-tion of acetylcholinesterase in the frontal isocortex of psychotic and nonpsychotic patients. *Arch. Neurol. Psychiat. 68:* 425 (1952).

14. McGEER, P. L., E. G. McGEER, and W. C. GIBSON. Aromatic excre-tory pattern of schizophrenics. *Science 123:* 1029 (1956).

15. RIEGELHAUPT, L. M. Investigations on the glyoxylic acid reactions on urines from schizophrenics and other psychotic patients. *J. nerv. ment. Dis. 123:* 383 (1956).

16. McGEER, P. L., E. G. McGEER, and J. E. BOULDING. Relation of aro-matic amino acids to excretory pattern of schizophrenics. *Science 123:* 1078 (1956).

17. BOGOCH, S. Effect of synthetic diet low in aromatic amino acids on schizophrenic patients. *Arch. Neurol. Psychiat. 78:* 539 (1957).

18. CAFRUNY, E. J., and E. F. DOMINO. Urinary excretion of some prod-ucts of tryptophan metabolism in schizophrenic patients. *Arch. Neurol. Psychiat. 77:* 336 (1958).

19. ALTSCHULE, M. D., E. P. SIEGEL, and D. H. HENNEMAN. Blood gluta-thione level in mental disease before and after treatment. *Arch. Neurol. Psychiat. 67:* 64 (1952).

20. LEACH, B. E., and R. G. HEATH. The in vitro oxidation of epinephrine in plasma. *Arch. Neurol. Psychiat. 76:* 444 (1956).

21. MARTENS, S., B. E. LEACH, R. G. HEATH, and M. COHEN. Glutathione levels in mental and physical illness. *Arch. Neurol. Psychiat. 76:* 630 (1956).

22. LEACH, B. E., M. COHEN, R. G. HEATH, and S. MARTENS. Studies in the role of ceruloplasmin and albumin in adrenalin metabolism. *Arch. Neurol. Psychiat.* 76: 635 (1956).

23. AKERFELDT, S. Oxidation of DPP by serum from patients with mental disease. *Science 125:* 117 (1957).

24. ABOOD, L. G., F. A. GIBBS, and E. GIBBS. Comparative study of blood ceruloplasmin in schizophrenia and other disorders. *Arch. Neurol. Psychiat.* 77: 643 (1957).

25. HORWITT, M. K., J. B. MEYER, A. C. MEYER, C. C. HARVEY, and D. HAFFRON. Serum copper and oxidase activity in schizophrenic patients. *Arch. Neurol. Psychiat.* 78: 275 (1957).

26. APRISON, M. H., and A. L. DREW. N,N-dimethyl-p-phenylenediamine oxidation by serum from schizophrenic children. *Science 127:* 758 (1958).

27. ANGEL, C., B. E. LEACH, S. MARTENS, M. COHEN, and R. G. HEATH. Serum oxidation tests in schizophrenic and normal subjects. *Arch. Neurol. Psychiat.* 78: 500 (1957).

28. HEATH, R. G., B. E. LEACH, L. W. BYERS, S. MARTENS, and C. A. FEIGLEY. Pharmacological and biological psychotherapy. *Amer. J. Psychiat. 114:* 683 (1958).

29. OSTFELD, A. M., L. G. ABOOD, and D. A. MARCUS. Studies with ceruloplasmin and a new hallucinogen. *Arch. Neurol. Psychiat.* 79: 317 (1958).

30. HEATH, R. G., S. MARTENS, B. E. LEACH, M. COHEN, and C. ANGEL. Effect on behavior in humans with the administration of taraxein. *Amer. J. Psychiat. 114:* 14 (1957).

31. HEATH, R. G., S. MARTENS, B. E. LEACH, M. COHEN, and C. A. FEIGLEY. Behavioral changes in nonpsychotic volunteers following the administration of taraxein, the substance obtained from serum of schizophrenic patients. *Amer. J. Psychiat. 114:* 917 (1958).

32. BLEULER, E. *Dementia Praecox or the Group of Schizophrenias.* New York: International Universities Press, Inc., 1950.

33. WOOLLEY, D. W. Serotonin in mental disorders. In *Hormones, Brain Function and Behavior.* (Ed. H. Hoagland) New York: Academic Press, Inc., 1957.

34. BRODIE, B. B., A. PLETSCHER, and P. A. SHORE. Evidence that serotonin has a role in brain function. *Science 122:* 968 (1955).

35. PLETSCHER, A., P. A. SHORE, and B. B. BRODIE. Serotonin as a mediator of reserpine action in brain. *J. Pharmacol. exp. Therapeut. 116:* 84 (1956).

36. BRODIE, B. B., J. S. OLIN, R. G. KUNTZMAN, and P. A. SHORE. Possible interrelationship between release of brain nor-epinephrine and serotonin by reserpine. *Science 125:* 1293 (1957).

37. BRODIE, B. B., and P. A. SHORE. On a role for serotonin and nor-epinephrine as chemical mediators in the central autonomic nervous system. In *Hormones, Brain Function and Behavior.* (Ed. H. Hoagland) New York: Academic Press, Inc., 1957.

37a. SELYE, HANS. *The Stress of Life.* New York: McGraw-Hill Book Company, Inc., 1956.

38. PINCUS, G., H. HOAGLAND, H. FREEMAN, F. ELMADJIAN, and L. P. ROMANOFF. A study of pituitary-adrenocortical function in normal and psychotic men. *Psychosom. Med. 11:* 74 (1949).

39. PINCUS, G., and H. HOAGLAND. Adrenal cortical responses to stress in normal men and in those with personality disorders. *Amer. J. Psychiat. 106:* 641 (1950).

40. HOAGLAND, H., G. PINCUS, F. ELMADJIAN, L. ROMANOFF, H. FREEMAN, J. HOPE, J. BALLAN, A. BERKELEY, and J. CARLO. Study of adrenocortical physiology in normal and schizophrenic men. *Arch. Neurol. Psychiat. 69:* 470 (1953).

41. BLISS, E. L., C. J. MIGEON, C. H. H. BRANCH, and L. T. SAMUELS. Adrenocortical function in schizophrenia. *Amer. J. Psychiat. 112:* 358 (1955).

42. HOAGLAND, H., M. RINKEL, and R. W. HYDE. Adrenocortical function and urinary phosphate excretion. *Arch. Neurol. Psychiat. 73:* 100 (1955).

43. RINKEL, M., R. W. HYDE, H. C. SOLOMON, and H. HOAGLAND. Experimental psychiatry II: Clinical and physio-chemical observations in experimental psychosis. *Amer. J. Psychiat. 111:* 881 (1955).

44. HENNEMAN, D. H., M. D. ALTSCHULE, and R. M. GONCZ. Carbohydrate metabolism in brain disease II, glucose metabolism in schizophrenic, manic-depressive and involutional psychoses. *Arch. intern. Med. 94:* 402 (1954).

45. HENNEMAN, D. H., M. D. ALTSCHULE, and R. M. GONCZ. Carbohydrate metabolism in brain disease III, fructose metabolism in schizophrenic, manic-depressive and involutional psychoses. *Arch. Neurol. Psychiat. 72:* 696 (1954).

46. HENNEMAN, D. H., M. D. ALTSCHULE, and R. M. GONCZ. Carbohydrate metabolism in brain disease IV, effect of hydrocortisone and corticotropin on the metabolic effects of administered glucose in patients with chronic schizophrenic and manic-depressive psychoses. *Arch. intern. Med. 95:* 241 (1955).

47. HENNEMAN, D. H., M. D. ALTSCHULE, R. M. GONCZ, and P. DAVIS. Carbohydrate metabolism in brain disease V, effect of epinephrine on intermediary carbohydrate metabolism in schizophrenic and manic-depressive psychoses. *Arch. intern. Med. 95:* 594 (1955).

48. ALTSCHULE, M. D., D. H. HENNEMAN, P. HOLLIDAY, and R. M. GONCZ. Carbohydrate metabolism in brain disease VI, lactate metabolism after infusion of sodium d-lactate in manic-depressive and schizophrenic psychoses. *Arch. intern. Med. 98:* 35 (1956).

49. ALTSCHULE, M. D., D. H. HENNEMAN, P. D. HOLLIDAY, and R. M. GONCZ. Carbohydrate metabolism in brain disease VII, the effect of glutathione on carbohydrate intermediary metabolism in schizophrenic and manic-depressive psychoses. *Arch. intern. Med. 99:* 22 (1956).

4

The Body Image in the Schizophrenic Reaction

LAWRENCE C. KOLB [1]

Over the years there have been various attempts to discuss schizophrenia in the psychosomatic context. Dr. S. Arieti suggests that the emotional disorder in schizophrenia leads to biochemical disturbances which, in turn, result in functional disintegration of the usual neuronal patterns of action. Thus, as a consequence of intense anxiety, he conceives of short-circuiting activity with dissolution of cerebral cortical functioning that presumably underlies communication and symbolization for functioning at lower levels of neurophysiological organization.

Bellak finds the psychosomatic approach to schizophrenia in the recognition of its multifunctional origin. He emphasizes the fact that the etiological elements in different cases may be either markedly psychogenic or somatic but holds that all contain both. To him the search for the single causative factor has impeded the development of knowledge and understanding of the condition.

Both Arieti and Bellak depart from the common narrow usage of the term *psychosomatic* wherein it is limited to

[1] Professor and Chairman, Department of Psychiatry, Columbia University, College of Physicians and Surgeons, and Director, New York State Psychiatric Institute, New York City.
This paper was presented as a Discussion.

describe the inappropriate or pathologic functioning of the autonomic nervous system and the viscera as a consequence of psychologic stress and emotional response. Yet when one considers the broader and more inclusive definition of *psychosomatic disturbance,* as outlined by Lawrence Kubie some years ago, Arieti's and Bellak's viewpoints and the one particularly presented here do allow the ready consideration of schizophrenia in the psychosomatic context.

Kubie includes as psychosomatic those disturbances involving the organs of internal economy, the organs of so-called instinctual functioning, such as the mouth, genitals, and anus, and the body image. The psychosomatic includes, then, not only organ systems enervated by the autonomic nervous system but also those where control is maintained simultaneously by both voluntary and involuntary nervous activity, as well as the body image which derives principally from perceptual integrations within the sensorimotor nervous system. He would exclude from the area of psychosomatic relations the higher levels of human cerebral functioning, such as the relationship to society, communicative activities, orientation in space and time, capacity to organize and integrate the information provided from without, and perceptual and conative activities. The borderline between the psychosomatic conditions and the higher communicative and symbolic functions subtly merges, particularly in the area of the body-image problems.

In my opinion, body-image development in schizophrenia is its peculiarly distinctive psychosomatic problem. The occurrence of bodily sensations in schizophrenia has been well known since the time of Bleuler. More attention has been paid to the hypochondriacal and abnormal bodily sensations than to the schizophrenic's general concept of his body. The bodily sensations are often considered to be "correct percepts" of somatic processes which are misinterpreted by the patient in the course of his introverted interest in his own body, as expressed in the form of delusions, such as "the body is dead" or "the body has no feelings." The schizophrenic's conception of the body as ugly, unpleasant, or undesirable is infrequently mentioned. Neither are delusions in regard to his concept of his body as they correspond to reality commonly specified.

Before discussing the body-image evolution and its distortion in the schizophrenic process, it may be helpful to define more precisely what is meant by the *body image*. I have found it worthwhile to distinguish between *body percept* or *body schema* and *body concept,* although both are generally included within the term *body image.* The former represents the postural image resulting from these sensorimotor experiences and current sensations which provide one with a basic model of the body as it functions outside of central consciousness. This perceptual image modifies incoming sensory impulses and their localization on the body surface and forms the positioning matrix for the intricate and delicate motor activities. This postural model of the body brings about the possibility of projecting oneself beyond the limits of the body. A dramatic representation of the postural model is, of course, the phantom-limb syndrome which occurs following an amputation. The phantom represents perceptions of this model organized over the years, principally through incoming kinesthetic and tactile perception, which remain in spite of the loss of the bodily part.

In contrast to the perceptual image, the conceptual image includes that which concerns the thoughts, feelings, and memories which evolve as the individual (ego) views his own body. Paul Schilder pointed out that the developing ego takes a view of the body as an object toward which it has perceptions, thoughts, and feelings. The distinction between the conceptual image and the ego should be made. Essentially, the body image is that which is viewed and responded to, whereas the ego is the viewer.

J. R. Smythies, in England, also has come to consider the term *body image*, as it is currently used, as too vague. He has substituted other terms which refer essentially to various aspects of the image. I do not wish to go into his various subdefinitions here because they would only distract from the central point.

Szasz attempted to resolve the problem of the ego-body relationship by pursuing the thinking of Schilder. He made the suggestion that the ego relates itself not only to other people as objects but also to the body of the self as an object. To him, the ego may develop transferences to the body from other objects (persons). Continuing his argument, Szasz explained the genesis of bodily feelings in schizophrenia in the following way. With the loss of some significant person, the ego of the schizophrenic withdraws from personal objects and takes its own body as the only remaining object to which it can relate itself. The patient transfers to his own body the attitudes, feelings, and fantasies formerly belonging to others and perhaps those from the particular person lost. Yet now he also fears the loss of his own body since it is his only remaining object. His hypochondriacal reflections may represent this fear. He may even give up parts of his body and experience them as nonexistent: a means of solving the problem of the fear of their loss. This process may induce self-mutilation, as the schizophrenic's ego forces the body to conform to its current body image. Szasz's ideas are concerned, however, with the ego-body relationship in the psychology of the adult schizophrenic state. He gives no attention to the possibility of a fundamental defect in the development of the body image nor to the possible evolutionary processes that might contribute to such a defect.

My own interest in the importance of the body image was aroused in a study of amputation. At the time of this study, it was striking to note the contrasting concepts of their bodies of certain schizophrenic patients to those of a group of young amputees. In general, the young amputees with emotional disturbances had, prior to their loss, a more than satisfying concept of their bodies, which might be best designated as an *overvaluation*. Their families had stressed for them accomplishment through, and appreciation of, their bodies as a means of relating themselves to others and, in this, their aspirations were either relatively successful through athletic accomplishments in the boys or through physical attractiveness in the girls. On the other hand, the schizophrenic patients as a group appeared to have a concept of ugliness which seemed to come from family attitudes of disparagement, derogation, and unfavorable comparisons. In some instances this attitude had its origin in an appraisal of inherited or congenital body defects unacceptable to the parents. In others it represented the consequences of family attitudes or lack of acceptance of the body of the growing child. In physical accomplishments the child failed to meet expectations or was found lacking in comparison to parents or other idealized persons or siblings.

An important question concerning the developing body image of the future schizophrenic pertains to a possible failure of the developing nervous system during maturation which should reflect evidence of a defective perceptual body image. This is the position taken by Lauretta Bender in her studies of schizophrenia in childhood when she emphasized the body-image disturbance in these children.

What information do we have in regard to the development of the body image? From the evolutionary standpoint, the individual organizes his perceptual image through the integration of multiple perceptions, a process beginning with the early stages of development. The important initial sensory impressions are the kinesthetic and the tactile; the optical contributes later. The hand-to-mouth movements appearing initially in the fetus are the precursors of the complex face-hand relationship which follows after the birth, particularly the one which develops in the nursing and feeding process. With the progressive acquisition of motility, the newborn child acquires knowledge of his body from other impressions. The child begins to use his hands to explore his own body surfaces and to contact others. The infant's explorative movements of his hands over his own body, the hands in contact with the mother, and their use in projecting into space and grasping objects provide the primary sensations underlying the establishment of the perceptual model of the body. These are also the processes upon which are founded the beginnings of self-awareness, individuality, and a sense of ego. Also in this early period, important perceptions are felt from exposure to sensations through stimulation of self or others which arouse varying degrees of pleasure and displeasure. It is not necessary at this time to discuss the relative importance of these other sensory contributions to the development of the perceptual image of the body.

In addition to the modifications resulting from the developmental sensory influences, the concept of the body evolves from the social experiences of the individual. The socially determined qualities of the body in relation to significant persons in the family or home environment merge with the earlier experiences of the individual. Toward his body and its various parts, the child acquires social percepts, attitudes, and affects culminating from the interaction with his parents and other members of his social group. Thus the parents impart an indelible impression on the child's concept of his body and its functions: as good or bad, pleasing or repulsive, clean or dirty, or one of love or dislike.

From this very brief account of the developmental process, it is apparent that these varied processes lead to the development in the child of body percepts, body concepts, and of ego, all of which occur more or less simultaneously. It seems that the perceptual model of the body has its beginning at an earlier stage than the conceptual model. The latter must await the sense of personal awareness, the ability of differentiative self from others, and the capacity to form various discriminations in regard to body values. We know that even the perceptual part of the body is not very well established before the age of five, since children who are born with congenital aplasia of the limbs, or who have amputations before this period, do not have the capacity to form a phantom of the amputated limb as do older children or adults. I mention this as Eichhoff suggests that the static image of the body is formed at 7–10 months of age. She arrived at this conclusion from noting the time babies are able to show interest in viewing themselves in a mirror. If it can be accepted that a body-image disturbance is a regular phenomenon in schizophrenia (and clinical observations suggest that in the full-blown disorder it usually exists), important implications evolve relative to the early development of the child as well as to treatment needed.

There are now several tests which may be considered methods of examining the perceptual image of the body. Morris Bender's test of simultaneous stimulation of face and hand, usually used in the diagnosis of diffuse cerebral dysfunction, is one. In this test the subject is asked to indicate where he has been touched when simultaneous stimulation is given to several portions of the body. With this test the perceptual pattern of both normal and unhealthy children is one of face dominance, the child reporting a touch on the face above and beyond that on the hand. By the age of seven nearly all normal children are able to perceive both face and hands stimuli within ten trials. On the other hand, Goldfarb and Pollack have found that many schizophrenic children are significantly different from normal children and from other children with nonschizophrenic behavior disorders, in that they fail to identify double simultaneous stimulation on face and hand even when tested with eyes open. Their patterns of perception with this test are similar to those seen in younger children and patients with mental changes due to severe brain damage. Such schizophrenic children generally show a retarded IQ measured by the Stanford-Binet test. In other words, a high proportion of the schizophrenic children show a perceptual defect related to body-image development. Some years ago, Szurek and his group stressed the preoccupation and puzzlement with their own mirror image of schizophrenic children. Evidence of a disturbance of the concept of the body in schizophrenia is well established through the studies of Machover and her students in the Draw-A-Person tests.

It is possible to consider the body-image disturbance of the schizophrenic patient, sometimes spoken of as *somatic delusion* or *depersonalization,* in a number of ways. One may think of the manifestation of a body-image disturbance in the adult as a regression to a bodily concept of infantile or childish life. But it appears much more likely that the body image of the schizophrenic patient has been distorted from the earliest period and represents essentially a disturbance in development of both the perceptual and conceptual images. The fact that the schizophrenic group of children are not homogeneous in this respect (as in Goldfarb's studies) is worthy of note. We do not have information from him in regard to the children's concept of their bodies. We have only the information concerning the responses on the face-hand test. It is possible that the children who responded well on the face-hand test were disturbed only in regard to the development of their body concepts rather than their body percept. The weakness of Goldfarb's study rests now on the fact that these schizophrenic children have not been followed to adulthood. We need to know by follow-up study whether we are concerned with the same process that is understood in later years as *schizophrenia.* It may well be that the differentiation of the several groups of children already heralds the great differences we see in our schizophrenic patient in adult life, i.e., those who are persistently and chronically ill and the other group who have a capacity for social adaptation. One might suggest that the schizophrenic child with a disturbance in his capacity to perceive the localization of objects on the body surface has a more serious maturational or developmental defect than those who do not show such a disordered function.

The significance of the body image as a psychosomatic expression of schizophrenia opens up a series of questions for which we have few observations and no answers at the moment. Is the body-image disturbance in schizophrenia the consequence of inherited structural or congenital defect in the development of the nervous system? Does this disturbance represent a dysfunction rather than a structural maldevelopment? Is this maldevelopment the consequence of disturbances in the communicative process between mother and child or, to put it another way, does the interaction between the mother's and the child's bodies, the mother's attitude and feelings as they are conveyed to the child in the very earliest times, lead to a disturbance in the capacity of the cortex to evolve a stable concept of the body, as well as altering later concepts of the body? If this is the case, what are the peculiarities of the mother-child relationship which contributes to the evolution of the disordered body-ego complex in the schizophrenic child? Is it that these children were not fondled enough, were not handled consistently, or were handled in a manner which produced such variables of sensory and emotional arousals that the cortex failed to integrate a stable body image?

In this symposium many of the succeeding papers will deal with the issues of communication in schizophrenia and the manner in which defective communicative systems or reliance on nonverbal systems impair the capacity for reality testing and the evolving of effective and socially adaptive behavior mechanisms. Little work is available which correlates the formation of the body concepts to intellectual and emotional growth. Yet it is within the framework of the early nonverbal interaction that the beginnings of visualization of others arise. Failure to form an image of one's own body impairs the capacity to form generalized images of others and is probably related to arrested development in abstract thinking. Impairment in the early communicative body-body relationship may well provide the defective foundation of the later contact of the schizophrenic with others. Goldfarb's interesting study of receptor preferences in schizophrenic children, in which he points out the avoidance of the use of distance receptors (vision and hearing) is important to the evolution of the body image in the sense that the totality of the image developing would thereby be limited. The schizophrenic children are seen by him to relate only to body parts—breast, skin, or warmth—explored through the contact receptors. This limitation of use of the distance receptors, which aid in facilitating the quick perception of total situations, leads apparently to the weakness of the schizophrenic ego in its inability to contact widely the world about him. The study of the distorted body-image evolution as it is related to primary perceptions is, to me, the major area of psychosomatic interest in schizophrenia and particularly in the area of the study of the early child-parent interaction, which is crucial to the understanding of the evolution of the communicative process. Herein must rest the beginnings of the basically stable and socially effective symbolic patterns and their distortions. The majority of studies currently in progress do not propose investigation of this area.

References

ARIETI, S. *Interpretation of Schizophrenia*. New York: Robt. Brunner, Inc., 1955.

ASCH, S. E., and H. A. WITKIN. Studies in space orientation. II. Perception of the upright with displaced visual fields and with the body tilted. *J. exp. Psycho.* 38: 455–477 (1948).

BELLAK, L. *Dementia Praecox.* New York: Grune & Stratton, Inc., 1948.

BENDER, M. D. *Disorders in Perception.* Springfield, Ill.: Charles C Thomas, Publisher, 1952.

BENNETT, D. I. Perception of the upright in relation to body image. *J. ment. Sci.* 102: 487–507 (1956).

BYSCHOWSKI, GUSTAV. Disorders of the body images in the clinical pictures of the psychoses. *J. Nerv. Ment. Dis.* 97: 310–335 (1943).

CLARK, W. E. LEGROS. Sensory experience and brain structure. *J. ment. Sci.* 104: 1–13 (1958).

EICHHOFF, L. F. W. Etiology of schizophrenia in childhood. *J. ment. Sci.* 98: 229–234 (1952).

FEDERN, P. *Ego Psychology and the Psychoses.* (Ed. E. Weiss) New York: Basic Books, Inc., 1953.

GOLDFARB, W. Infant rearing and problem behavior. *Amer. J. Orthopsychiat.* 13: 249–265 (1945).

GOLDFARB W. Effect of psychological deprivation in infancy and subsequent stimulation. *Amer. J. Psychiat.* 102: 18–33 (1945).

KOLB, L. C. *The Painful Phantom. Psychology, Physiology and Treatment.* Springfield, Ill.: Charles C Thomas, Publisher, 1954.

KOLB, L. C. Disturbances of the body image. In *American Handbook of Psychiatry.* (Ed. S. Arieti) New York: Basic Books, Inc. (to be published).

SCHILDER, PAUL. *The Image and Appearance of the Human Body. Studies in the Constructive Energies of the Psyche.* Psyche Monographs, 4. London: George Routledge & Sons, Ltd., 1935.

SMYTHIES, J. R. The experience and description of the human body. *Brain* 76: 132–145 (1953).

SZASZ, T. C. *Pain and Pleasure.* New York: Basic Books, Inc., 1957.

SZASZ, T. C. The psychology of bodily feelings in schizophrenia. *Psychosom. Med.* 19: 11–16 (1957).

SZUREK, S. Childhood schizophrenia, psychotic episodes and psychotic maldevelopment. *Amer. J. Orthopsychiat.* 26: 519–543 (1956).

WITKEN, H. *Personality through Perception.* New York: Harper & Brothers, 1954.

5

Contribution of Linguistic-Kinesic Studies to the Understanding of Schizophrenia

RAY L. BIRDWHISTELL[1]

It would be presumptuous at this stage of the game, to suggest that the linguistic-kinesic methodologies have contributed much more than documentation of, or checking devices for, already prevalent insights. Certainly the conception that mental illness represents some kind of communication disorder is as old as organized psychiatry. Within the field of anthropology, the work of Margaret Mead and Gregory Bateson on the Balinese in the thirties is a forthright statement of this point of view. Yet it seems fair to say that the linguistic-kinesic (L-K) approach is more than a rechewing of already well-masticated, if not already digested, material. Perhaps in the reexamination of what we mean by *communication,* we can get a clearer picture of what we mean by *disordered* communication. First we shall consider communication as a social event and disorder within it as a social disturbance. If little emphasis is placed here on traditional psychological mechanisms, it is because such mechanisms seem to be irrelevant to this discussion.

[1] Associate Professor, Department of Anthropology, and Coordinator, Institute for Research in Human Communication, University of Buffalo, New York.

However, this is no attempt to preempt the analysis of schizophrenia for the anthropologist or the sociologist, much less for the kinesicist or the linguist. It is perfectly clear that research in schizophrenia must proceed at a variety of levels: genetic, chemical, neurological, and psychological. Any acquaintance with the growing body of data on schizophrenia leaves one impressed with the fact that there are probably genetic predispositions to mental illness which leave the organism cocked, as it were, to go off if the conditions for emergence are present to a critical degree. We do not pretend that in the L-K approach we have somehow gained sufficient control of the data to discuss the mechanism of the triggering of the explosion. Neither do we suggest that we have invented either some kind of muffler which prevents the explosion or a clinical magic which puts the pieces back together again. It does seem, however, that the L-K approach constitutes a research technique which may make possible the slowing down of these events so that they can be studied. Perhaps, as such studies proceed, we shall be able to order the disorder to the point that we can understand and interfere with it.

Our study of schizophrenia, then, is dependent upon that section of the universe with which our tools bring us into contact. And our tools are specially constructed for dealing with the social system and for measuring the social events which lie within this system. Research concerned with that social system, communication, should develop control over an order of data with important implications for workers on other levels of research with schizophrenia. But, *as data*, the events with which we are concerned have their analytic reality on the social level. One psychiatrist has said that schizophrenia is a physiological disease whose symptoms appear to disrupt society. This seems no more definitional than saying that schizophrenia is a social disease with physical symptoms. As a nonmedically trained researcher, I am quite content to take the diagnosed schizophrenic and study him as a node, or, rather, a particular kind of warp in the communicational system. But, for the purposes of this paper, schizophrenia represents a particular class of communicational disturbance.

Drs. Fromm-Reichmann and Brosin have made it clear that schizophrenia is, as presently defined, no all-or-nothing disease. They have made it clear that for many, some degree of schizophrenia is "a way of life." This is not to anticipate Mr. Bateson's paper, but it seems evident that the hospitalization of a schizophrenic is not only a statement concerning serious illness on the part of the patient but also is a measure of the tolerance of the family and community for dealing with disturbances of this order. The schizophrenic under treatment constitutes evidence, then, not only for some order of illness, but also for some kind of interactional failure on the part of the nonclinical society. It is true that some physicians have greater success with schizophrenics than do others. A number of "explanations" have been offered for this special success rate—"explanations" which would require clinical competence to evaluate. The central thesis of all seem to be the same, however. The successful therapist is a man (or woman) who is able to make and sustain meaningful contact with his patient—in other words, to engage in directed communication with him. In this sense, the therapist represents a special social invention in applied communication.

It is obvious that if we were to be able to comprehend the nature of such successful therapy, if we were able to isolate the skills which make possible this reordered communication, then we should have increased knowledge of the nature of the illness itself. At least, if we understood the therapeutic structure, we might be better able to teach others to participate in it. And in order better to understand this special kind of interaction, we must have extensive research of a very specialized nature. For such research to be more than impressionistic description (by however sensitive observers), devices for objective analysis are necessary. Intuitive description or self-appraisal are far from trivial in psychiatric research. They have, in fact, provided the basis for most of our present knowledge. The fact does remain, however, that skill in engaging in communication with psychotics is not always accompanied by skill in communicating with oneself or one's colleagues. Just as advances in physiology and chemistry have made it possible to objectify and expand clinical insights in pathology and medicine, it is hoped that linguistics and kinesics will make possible a new level of objectification in psychiatric research.

Without going further into the methodologies, let us say that kinesics and linguistics make it possible to analyze exhaustively the communicational aspects of verbal and body-movement behavior of human beings in an interaction situation. Thus a sound film of successful therapy would provide a wealth of raw data, which, if properly sifted and assessed, should provide us with extensive objective cues as to the course of the therapeutic process. If we also had films of less successful therapeutic contacts to put into contrast with this, we might indeed be able to gain insight into what constitutes significant interaction with schizophrenics. Yet, if we are realistic, the fantastic cost of such filming and the even more fantastic cost of the analysis—assuming we had the analytic manpower for such a task (which we do not at present have) —make this an almost useless research design. The sheer recognition of the fact that successful therapy has something to do with communication, however, provides us with a base line from which to operate. As one therapist put it, "If you can reach them and hold them, you can remit them." This seems to indicate that the primary problem of dealing therapeutically with schizophrenics is the problem of establishing sufficiently effective contact that the patient accepts or at least becomes again part of conventional systems of inter-action to the point that the society can deal with him. Obviously, the more explicit we can become about the communication system, the more likely are we to be able to report the critical moments in the psychiatric process and the more likely is the therapist to be able to respond to the appeals of his patients and to make his wishes known to them. Although it may not at present be feasible to employ kinesicists or linguists to analyze extensive films of therapy in search for the secret of communicating with schizophrenics, it may very well be possible to equip psychiatrists with sufficient insight into the nature of the communicational process to make their own intuitions explicit and thus more available to their colleagues.

To be more explicit about the word *communication,* as used here, will make clearer the relationship between kinesics and linguistics and the study of disordered human interaction. In popular usage the term *communication* has occupied the somewhat anomalous position of being used both as a synonym for people talking to one another and as a cover term for newspapers, radios, telegraphy, and the like. In both these usages, either a mentalistic or mechanistic folk model has governed the definition of the word. This model includes (1) a sending set: a radio, a printing press, a telegraph key, or a brain with a mouth attached; (2) a receiving set of some kind which would include a brain with an ear attached; and (3) a message carried by some medium which comes out of (1) and goes into (2). With such a model the analysis of communication is concerned with en-coding, decoding, and the "noise" which prevents what is encoded from being received properly for decoding. And unfortunately, many who use this model act as though they were dealing with machines. Therapy becomes a matter of oiling, greasing, cutting out a part, or putting in a rheostat. The model becomes the man and the therapist the machinist.

Although tremendous contributions have been made by the cyberneticists and other information theorists to our knowledge of systems, informational theory is not the point here. If this is made clear from the beginning considerable misunderstanding can be avoided.

The term *communication,* as used in this discussion, is a term which is related to the dynamic, patterned interaction of the membership of a social group. As such, communication is constituted *from* the learned and patterned utilization of the various sensory modalities. Through this patterned participation the membership of a group is incorporated into a given society's ways of dealing with the universe. Thus, an individual does not communicate; he engages in or becomes part of communication. He may move, or make noises, he may emit odors, he may emit certain chemicals, or he may resist pressure—but he does not communicate. In a parallel fashion, he may see, he may hear, smell, taste, or feel—but he does not communicate. In other words, he does not originate communication; he participates in it. Communication as a system, then, is not to be understood on a simple model of action and reaction, however complexly stated. As a system, it is to be comprehended on the transactional level.

This does not mean that the analysis of such a system delivers data of no import for the understanding of individual behavior. Quite the contrary. Only when we have sufficient comprehension of this system can we hope to evaluate the apparent warps within it. Only as we can separate simple permissible variations in the internal behavior of this system can we hope to have more than the most impressionistic and ethnocentric awareness of its points of strain. To be more blunt: the statistics as to the incidence of schizophrenia merely make more secure the assumption that schizophrenia is evidence of social malfunction.

The individual is not a black box with one orifice for emitting a hunk of stuff called *communication* and another for receiving it. At the same time communication is not simply the sum of the bits of information which pass between two people in a given period of time.

Let us suppose that some wealthy and benevolent foundation was impressed with the fact that the human organism is a fantastically sensitive system capable of receiving literally hundreds of thousands of bits of information and became so concerned with the implications of this that they were willing to support extended research into the nature of the interconnections between this organism and the remainder of the universe. Let us further imagine that we decided to make up an experimental *univers à deux* and put two human beings in an elaborate box, and then decided to record all the informational signal units that flowed into the box and were potentially receivable by its occupants. Theoretically, the various machines would feed to a master tape some 2,500–5,000 bits (and up to about 10,000) of information per second. These recorded bits are notations of minimally discernible changes in the sound, light, and odor stream. Obviously their identity as units is dependent on the refinements of the recording devices. However we refine it, we are already swamped by the flood of data. And if we were to play this game of astronomical numbers to its awe-ful end, probably the lifetime efforts of roughly half the adult population of the United States would be required to sort the units deposited on one tape record in the course of an hour's interaction between the two subjects! Nor is there any comfort in the thought of Univac's speedy digestive system. Univac could deliver stacks of counted units and further stacks of correlations, but at this level that is all we would have—stacks of figures. This kind of practical infinity play is all the more depressing if we are tough enough scientists to know that we deal with an interdependent universe which cannot include accidental, isolated, or finally meaningless units. Something is always happening, but if we just count signals, it has no more value than if nothing were happening. If we had to stop our studies at this point we might just as well go back to an atomistic and mentalistic model of a human being as a *Ding an sich*. With such a model we are condemned to do our research on little balloons full of words which are somehow framed or filled out by gesticulation which we could dignify although not clarify by calling *nonverbal communications*.

Fortunately, however, we do not have to engage in such elaborate census taking in order systematically to analyze human interaction any more than we have to isolate and tag every molecule of water in order to do hydrography. All we need to do to make communication research efficient, manageable, and meaningful is to construct a methodology which will enable us to order our record so that we can isolate from it the testably significant classes of events. Now for the word *methodology*. Obviously as human beings we are continually engaged in abstracting, recording, and evaluating the communicational events of our environment. This process of interaction must not be confused with the process of scientific observation. There is no need to carry coals to this psychiatric Newcastle. Anthropologists are grateful for confirmation of the observation that only a small portion of one's behavior is subject to recall, that one is aware of only a small part of his behavior. As students of exotic societies, anthropologists are painfully conscious of the fact that one's observations are limited by his own past experience. Or, to state it differently, the environment is always strained through internalized categorization devices. And unless we can develop a methodology which permits of objective evaluation, the shape of the events which we abstract from the external environment will undoubtedly have the shape of the biasing screen of our own cultural experience. To be a member of one's culture, one must learn what and how to perceive and how and what not to perceive. And the productive deviancy of the insightful perceiver is hard to come by. Thus, by and large, even the best intentioned observation is a cultural performance and, unless explicitly channelized, will tend toward moral perception, cognition, and rationalization.

This is not to deny that many generalizations which we are now deriving from our data were long ago contributed by skilled and intuitive, even artistic, observers who somehow through special experience and training gained control of their sensitivity to a degree that they tore off sections of their cultural blinders. There were, after all, men in early Greece who could phrase the universe in terms directly translatable into Einsteinian formulations. Such insights remained at the best unpopular bits of poetry until metaphysics, research, mathematics, and technology were sufficiently advanced to make them commonplace within the experimental reach of the average college senior today.

In other words, even the most motivated observer who abstracts from the behavioral stream remains an artist until he can describe the operations whereby he abstracts his units. And this is only the first step in the data-ordering process. If we are to test his operations and to test the significance he assigns to each piece of data, he must give us explicit instructions which make it possible for us to duplicate his operations. And this is precisely what linguistics and kinesics are designed to do. These are methods whereby the infracommunicational systems can be explicitly studied and compared and whereby the events isolated through their methodologies can be put into perspective. The primary contribution which the linguistic-kinesic approach has to make lies in its objectification of interactional behavior. These methodologies permit the reduction of the data to significant units. Their analytic procedure permits us to recognize customary and predictable assemblages of such units and thus to recognize with maximal efficiency those deviations from expectancy which are so significant for diagnostic or prognostic endeavor.

The important point of all this is *methodology*. The analytic procedure does not create body movement or speech. These are natural systems which our methodology permits us to objectify to the point of manipulation. More than two thousand years of study of language have both deceived us and given us insight into the nature of speech and language. These years of research, climaxed by the past two or three decades of linguistic-frontier crossing—occasioned by exceptional experimental rigor and vigor—make it possible for us to leave that period of humanistic historicity which left many with such a false impression of the nature of language and, by extension, with such a misconception of communication, that its study provided but few sharp instruments for the practitioner's tool kit. In general, a product of the literate scholar's overpreoccupation with literacy and with a set of rules for verbal etiquette (grammar), the conception of language held until recently is so deceptive that it may be useful to review certain aspects relevant to this discussion. This is hardly the place to set forth the technical theory or the methodological procedures of linguistics or kinesics.[2]

The author's research concern with schizophrenia has been largely occasioned by work with the psychiatrists Brosin and Fromm-Reichmann, the ethnologist Bateson, and the linguists McQuown, Hockett, and, particularly, Smith and Trager. Beginning with the study of Doris and Billy at the Center for Advanced Study in the Behavioral Sciences at

[2] See "The Natural History of an Interview" which should soon be in print and which contains much of the technical information which would flesh out this discussion.

Palo Alto, I have continued since that time to be largely concerned with the study of the parent-child context. Thus the discussion here is centered around the introduction of the child into the communication system of the society and the implications of this for the study of schizophrenia. If the discussion is overgeneral or too programmatic, this very inadequacy will perhaps make manifest the need for research in this area.

The work of the ethnologists and comparative psychologists in the last few years has forced us to reevaluate our previous conceptions of the relationship between human and animal behavior. Many of us marveled at the intricacies of the associations (which we termed *genetically determined* and let it go at that) which are present in insect societies. We looked at apes and studied them somatically as carrying clues which might give us insight into the evolution of man. But, because of the nature of our theory and the tremendously difficult task of making sustained and checkable observations, we were largely concerned with watching the behavior of individual animals. We described them as operating in groups, or herds, or prides, or flocks and in anthropomorphic amazement projected upon them certain human characteristics, most of which were individually psychological in nature. Recently, however, we have been forced to review if not completely to revamp these conceptions. With the work of Tinbergen, of Hess, of Lorenz, of Blauvelt, and others, it has become increasingly evident that social living is an adaptational imperative for the membership of many nonhuman species. As we became willing to forego simplistic arguments concerning heredity and, or rather versus, environment and turned to the behavioral description of critical developmental moments in the individual's life, atomistic theoretics began to give way before more dynamic system models.

These insights, plus the theoretical and technical achievements of the linguist and the kinesicist, in a new experimental world made possible by the sound camera, the slow-motion analyzer, and the tape recorder, have forced us to a reevaluation of evolution. Such a reevaluation has carried with it a new perspective on what we mean by *human behavior*—and by extension what is significant about the patterned interdependence of human beings. If we are willing to concede that the evolutionary ladder runs from the inorganic to the organic to the social and, finally, to the human, we shall probably also be willing to reevaluate our primary postulates as to the nature of man himself. Certainly we may find ourselves in a position which makes less conscionable any isolation of disease and particularly mental disease within man's epidermatic frontiers. We are ready to look with new eyes at the life history of an individual and to ask new questions about the violence we do when we act as though we deal with a preformationalistically dominated personality made of plastic and which is shaped by isolated traumatic events.

Who knows how any given member of *Homo sapiens* internalizes the conventional understandings of his social group to the extent that his social behavior is by and large predictable? Yet, even the sketchiest survey of human societies reveals that he does this. There is little solace in a so-called "learning theory," although one is impressed with the brilliance of the learning experimentalist who can create a training situation in which human beings can be persuaded to deal with new information in a manner analogous to that apparently employed by white rats or Grey Walter's machines. The fact remains that infants from every society in the world can and *do* internalize the communicational system of that society in approximately the same amount of time that the "normal" six-year-old in every society is able to move smoothly within the communication system of his society. There is no need to become involved in arguments for gestalt versus associational or any other model of learning. The discussion to follow will perhaps be clearer, however, if some of the conceptions, which the author's preliminary acquaintance with children in the communicational context has led him to hold, are made clear. It is indeed true that years of carefully ordered observation and analysis of children in the learning situation are necessary before the mechanism of this incorporation becomes clear. Yet the traditional learning experiment apparatus does seem inapplicable for this study. We cannot study the social behavior of a fish by taking him out of water.

The child is born into a society already keyed for his coming. A system exists into which he must be assimilated if the society is to sustain itself. If his behavior cannot, after a period of time, become predictable to a degree expected in that society, he must be specially treated. In some societies the nonassimilator will be allowed to die; in others he may be given a special institutional position. This special treatment can range from deification to incarceration. But ultimately the goal is the same: to make his behavior sufficiently predictable that the society can go about the rest of its business.

From a different point of view, depending upon the society's expectancy structure, the child must in a given period of time learn how to learn what the society expects of him, how to inform responsible members of that society what he has learned and, at the same time, learn to use them as sources of new learning. Perhaps even more fundamental than this, his very survival depends upon his receiving and sending certain orders of message from and to those about him. The Spitz babies, like the Blauvelt kids and lambs, provide us with all too clear insights into the fact that the organism must receive certain kinds of stimulating experiences or it dies. We can combine the results of these suggestive experiments with the data provided by the sensory-deprivation studies and evaluate this insight in the light of our increasing knowledge about the complexity of the perceptive process. This outline of the problem of bringing a new member into society reveals a process so critical and complex that even the least impressionable student is inclined to wonder how we make it at all. This process is commonplace for every society. Yet the fact that we are here discussing this matter is testament to the fact that the process is not always successful.

We know so little about the dimensions of biological or social time that we cannot say whether the infant and the society have a long or short time in which to accomplish the basic task of incorporation. We know only that it must be done and that some societies act as though there were very little time for this task while others do not even conceive of it as a problem. We may, however, make this generalization: in every society, before attaining membership in that society, the child must gain control of the pattern of, and be incorporated into the communication system of the society. And, to repeat, in every society we know anything about, at least in so far as language is concerned, this occurs by the time the child is six years old. Now to state explicitly what was implied before: gaining control of language is not the simple accumulation of an aggregate of words; it is not the possession of a certain sized vocabulary. Nor is the control of that infracommunicational system, body motion, made up of memorizing a list of facial expressions or gestures. Communication control is not achieved through a simple additive process which involves the accumulation of parcels of sounds or body motion which carry encapsulated chunks of meaning. Nor is it the but slightly more complex matter of hooking together these pieces called *words* and *gestures* into little meaning trains called *sentences*. I use the word *simple* here in derision, for if this were the way we had to incorporate our communicational system, the human life span would not be long enough to permit us ever to achieve such control. Human culture is possible because we do not have to do it this way—because we learn in a patterned way.

Look for a moment at the pitifully little that is known about the rate and sequence of human language and motion incorporation. When I say "pitifully little," however, I imply no apology. Recent developments in linguistics and paralinguistics, in kinesics and parakinesics at last makes possible the systematic descriptive analysis of this developmental process. Even these few and very tentative descriptions, gathered from all too little observation, make it possible for us to envision a day when we can objectively analyze the communication behavior of a particular child and prognosticate as to his ability to adapt to his communicational milieu. For the linguistic material I rely on the observations of Smith and Trager, modified by discussion with Hockett and McQuown, and strained through my own conceptions which are, at least in part, the result of kinesic observation.

The number of sounds distinguishable from each other that the so-called vocal apparatus can make may run into the thousands, depending upon the instruments used for delineating them. The possible combinations of these is beyond the number of atoms postulated for the universe. Yet we need not trouble ourselves with these possibility figures. The fact of the matter is that while societies choose different segments and sections of the range, phoneticians have found no society whose significant phonologic sounds could not be described from a set of 42 basic positional symbols each modifiable by from five to ten marks which indicate special placement or release. And to do phonemic analysis, which deals with the least meaningful classes of sounds used by any language, even fewer symbols may be required. Trager has said that no society that he knows anything about has less than fifteen of such basic units nor many more than fifty.

The number of phonemes in the repertoire of any given society does not seem to mean very much about the complexity of that society. In our own we utilize 45 which includes nine vowels, three semivowels, twenty-one consonants, four stresses, four pitches, and four junctures.

Comparably, while the human face alone is capable of making some 250,000 different expressions, I have fifteen placement symbols plus eleven special markers sufficient to record the significant positions of all the faces I have seen. Less than one hundred symbols are all that are required to deal with any kinesic subject which I have yet studied—and this recording covers the activity of the whole body in its through-time activity.

The human infant is an amoral mass of wrigglings and vocalizing; it lives in a milieu of moral speakers and movers. By the age of six it will be a moral vocalizer, that is, it will have reduced its range of noises to that narrow list employed by the members of his milieu. I am not sure when he becomes a moral wriggler, although there is every indication that adolescence (and here generalization is restricted to North American culture) marks a period in which the wriggling becomes restrained into moral limits. The difference between the kinesic and linguistic system probably related to the fact that although body-motion communicational behavior is just as much learned behavior as is language behavior, we simply have not, heretofore, known enough about it to teach it. That is, parents and peers have the range and structure of the phonemic system sufficiently in awareness to direct and more or less explicitly rectify the behavior of the young speaker. Yet this teaching aspect should not be overstressed. It is said that the apparently incoherent babbling of a six-month-old is already sufficiently structured that a French baby will have a predominance of French phonemes and an American baby a predominance of those characteristic of American English. I have not watched enough babies from enough different societies to make a similar generalization about their respective kinesic repertoires.

All this discussion has been about very old babies, because by the time a baby is a year old he has already gained some acquaintance and, I am tempted to say, control of large portions of the cross-referencing phenomena which will make his language a pattern system and the incorporation of which will make him a patterned learner of the details to follow. By the age of six weeks he begins to respond fairly systematically to the vocal qualifiers used by the children and adults who verbalize around him. These include particular variations in intensity and pitch height and in extent variation, which would include drawl and clipping. Again, research in kinesic phenomena is too limited to permit our determining what is systematically reacted to by the child. Although I do not have the experimental data to support it, I am inclined to believe that the child comes to comprehend his kinesic qualifier behavior and his vocalization behavior, which includes the vocal qualifiers and the vocal characterizers, in a full package. The vocal characterizers, incidentally, include that patterned behavior which encases language: such as, giggling, snickering, whimpering, sobbing, yelling, whispering, moaning, groaning, whining, breaking, belching, and yawning. There is no time to demonstrate that these are structured by each society in its paralinguistic and parakinesic system. However, these phenomena *are* patterned and *are* learned. It requires very little observation to see that at least by the age of two the child has considerable comprehension of what the mother is doing when he cannot see her and what she feels about what she is saying when he can only see her.

We are getting too far ahead of the developmental picture. There is reason to believe that by the age of four months the child is responding to the intonation patterns of the language and that by the age of nine months, if not already talking in partial sentences, he is usually babbling in his language's intonation pattern and engaging in some kinemorphs at least characteristic of the children of his group. The range of using meaningful morphemes, words, is considerable. We have reports of children as young as five months saying "mama" or other clumps of phonemes which the parents respond to as meaningful symbolizations. On the other hand, even extremely bright children may not begin to talk until well into the third or fourth year, sometimes breaking their self-imposed silence with appallingly sophisticated statements. A similar story seems to prevail for little movers. If we use eye focus as a marker for the presence of complex kinemorphic constructions, we see some children who maintain "overwide focus" well into kindergarten—and some females look as though even marriage will not make them forego it! On the other hand, I have seen children who began this kind of communicative focus behavior as early as the tenth month. I realize that "overwide focus" doesn't convey much meaning. By "overwide focus" is meant the open-eyed contemplation of others that infants have which gives them the look that somehow they are looking out from behind their eyes.

Even with our present limited knowledge about the process, which admittedly has been gathered by a dual process of limited observation and questionable extrapolation backward from the behavior of older children, we can generalize that the child learns his communication behavior through the incorporation of a series of modifying and interlocking patterns. Intimately associated with his enculturation and socialization, his language and his motion system provide him with contact with the problems of his environment and often with their solutions. Through this system he finds out who he is in relation to others and what his expectancies and responsibilities are. In short, it is through the various modal-

ities of his communication system that he structures, antici-
pates, and is rewarded or failed by his environment.
Through out-of-awareness, but clearly discrete, signals does
he learn the directives, the prohibitions, the encouragements,
and the warnings which govern his consistent association
with other members of his society. His language and his
body-motion system are flexible and malleable, yet, at the
same time, they are adaptive and functional only because
they are so systematically organized. Not only do they
carry instructions and descriptions and responses—reaffirma-
tion of old understandings and directions which result in
the acceptance of new ones—but also these messages are
cross-referenced by statements about the messages themselves. For this insight I am particularly grateful to Bateson.
The messages are cross-referenced by explicit and analyzable
behavior which instructs as to whether the message is to be
taken literally or metaphorically, as a joke, or as an unavoid-
able prescription. These systems contain explicit instructions
as to the relationship between the speaker and the auditor
and are even so styled that a series of apparently contradictory messages can be put under a rubric which assembles
them as noncontradictory.

A recording sheet for the communicational behavior of
human beings requires at least 100 separate lines for each
actor. No item is nonfunctional; such a recording represents the course of an interaction of two or more human
beings playing out their adjustments and adaptations to each
other, to themselves, and to the larger universe. Its success
as a system depends upon the child's having been assimilated in a manner which permits a growing and positive
participation in the society. If we can comprehend the
systematic nature of this participation, it takes but little
imagination to see what can happen if this system is mis-
learned or inappropriately handled. So, to describe certain
aspects of schizophrenia as inappropriate communication, is

not to redefine schizophrenia; it is only to suggest an approach to the discovery of its genesis, its course of development, and hopefully, one approach to its amelioration, if not its cure.

I have talked about childhood because this is where I think the tendency toward schizophrenia is structured; the fact that it does not at times appear until later years may be a measure of the social environment and its stresses rather than of the period of social genesis.

Linguistics and kinesics, then, provide tools whereby the interactional behavior within a family can be abstracted and measured in manipulatable units. With these tools we can do research on an interaction in a manner which increases our ability to evaluate the interactional process. Further, we can use these to measure the therapeutic process and to evaluate the results of this process. In short, the L-K methodology shows promise as a clinical tool for diagnosis, description, and prognosis. It is clear that linguistics and kinesics make possible a level of objective research heretofore impossible. The real promise of these approaches, however, probably lies in the perspective with which they may, as research proceeds, provide us about the nature of the human personality. I am convinced that as we know more about how human beings interact, we shall also be able to engage in preventive work and be able to catch critical communication distortion earlier and take another step toward giving the schizophrenic full self-awareness, self-acceptance, and mental health.

Discussion

Henry W. Brosin [3]

I am sure that you share with me both admiration and respect for the speaker's skill in conveying clearly to us a

[3] Professor and Chairman, Department of Psychiatry, University of Pittsburgh School of Medicine, and Director, Western Psychiatric Institute and Clinic, Pittsburgh.

few difficult concepts and also for his modesty and caution in making claims about the methodology and techniques involved in this relatively new area. I say "relatively new" because many specialists in speech, grammar, language, logic, semantics, and body motion have been bringing order of some kind into the modes of human interaction for at least 2,000 years. Our current bibliography runs into many more titles. Dr. Birdwhistell has chosen to tell us of about a dozen propositions, at least six of which are major subjects, which may be of help to clinicians in understanding better the nature of the communication patterns in the group of schizophrenias. He has presented material about the basic concepts of communication and the technical devices which will eventually reveal much about the nature of these disorders as they occur in their natural setting, whatever the etiology may be.

It seems to me that the linguistic-kinesic analysis of behavior brings us back to a fundamental rule in clinical psychiatry, namely, to study the patient for clues for understanding his behavior. If we find ourselves in possession of improved tools and skills for such study, and if we also develop perspectives and insights which increase our awareness of what is happening to the patient and those around him, we can confidently expect better methods of prevention and control. If many of the schizophrenic groups are the result of faulty maturation—and we have no truly convincing evidence to the contrary at this time—it will serve us well as clinicians to use the natural history methods of Claude Bernard, Darwin, and Freud, not to mention hundreds of other pioneers in both the basic and clinical sciences.

With the advances we have heard about here, we can refine our methods, concepts, and experiments so that genuine verification becomes possible in place of the relatively crude subjective clinical recital, however brilliant and insightful it may be. It is necessary to be patient, since there are some things which cannot be hurried, but we can meanwhile help our experimental colleagues as much as possible as they move from exploratory phases of hypothesis generation to more systematic verification.

Perhaps it would be well to reassert that the linguistic-kinesic methods of analysis of human interaction or transaction follow the basic canons of belief in (1) a strict determinism, (2) a biological substrate dependent upon genetic transmission, and (3) a neurobiochemical and physiological organization which acts upon and is in turn, often rapidly, acted upon by factors from other levels of organization, including the psychological and social levels. The introduction of such activities as motivation, emotional states, and learning into the chemical and physiological experiments we have heard about will require better observation, better recording of all levels of messages, and better objective criteria for different events in an interaction sequence.

It is my belief that these linguistic-kinesic methods furnish a teaching and training ground for such objective recording and that there are immense possibilities inherent in multiple judges studying at length and at leisure the same material. We have reason to believe that "intuition" can be recorded, studied, and compared with various kinds of clinical and social science data which will make the bases for such insights intelligible.

It is also apparent from the work of Bateson and Birdwhistell that the application of these methods involves a family of hypotheses, some of them rather new and very much in active stages of "becomingness." It will not be easy to accept many of the observations until we have had time to see and review the evidence at first hand. It may be even more difficult to accept tentative and complex hypotheses which are in a state of flux. This meeting, however, is worthwhile because of the new work and concepts in chemistry and physiology as well as in the behavioral or human sciences. The possibilities for learning something new about the schizophrenias are now better than they ever were in the latter areas and I shall cite an example.

Bateson's films of schizophrenic families document how message transmission is ordered and disordered in systematic ways. Even though we do not know the relevance of many of these transactions, we can now record them with a degree of accuracy hitherto unattainable, particularly in subtle areas where we have not been able to observe a family in action intensively enough to describe the nature of the communication system in progress. Some of you may well wonder about the problem of redundancy, but we *need* more actual experience with numerous cases in several different cultures before the questions of selection and significance of material and the simplifications which may possibly accompany them can be judicially appraised.

Dr. George Preston told me of one schizophrenic patient who had been bottle fed by his mother while she held him inverted with his head between her knees and his legs upon her breasts. Most of us know of similar unconventional practices, which may or may not be the necessary and sufficient conditions for rearing schizophrenics; but now we have methods for close comparative study over various differentiated population groups which may provide clues to the basic processes involved. The enlarged concepts of transmission of signals in all modalities and at the various levels of organization in a family or group or an entire culture are a far advance over the relatively restricted history and mental-status examinations of two decades ago.

Many of you will recall studies of both the form and content of schizophrenic productions including transcriptions, recordings, association and projective tests, TAT, finger painting, and drawings. All these methods yield insight, even those such as Elliott Chapple and Saslow utilizing the content-free Interaction Chronograph. It is my belief that these are not comparable to the linguistic-kinesic methods or concepts in most respects and that it is a misunderstanding to attempt to use linguistic-kinesic methods as if they were something else. This is especially apparent in some papers in which excellent workers concentrate on counting techniques of the coding markers of various vocal or kinesic events and find that there is no significant correlation between them and the overt behavior. (L. Wynne and A. Dittman, American Psychiatric Association meeting, 1958.) They apply their technique of counting to the messages in their passage between sender and receiver. Both Bateson and Birdwhistell emphasize the necessity for keeping in mind that a message is not a message except as it is engaged with the sender and the receiver. Significance or meaning is inherent in the total system. Usually in human communication it is necessary to know a good deal about the total matrix of the communication system before one can define the "meaning" of a piece of behavior. It is usually necessary to know what the state of the system was before the particular message was sent; and often it is necessary to know at least a few of the future referents which are inherent in the current message in order to do proper decoding or interpretation. Unless the total process is kept in mind it is useless to try to study one fragment.

Some workers have said that science is necessarily digital in character and that therefore it is impossible to study the patterned behavior we are talking about. Some authors believe that verbal systems are largely digital and that the paralinguistic systems are largely analogic—continuous in character and therefore beyond digital analysis. This fits in with Dr. Worden's questions about the violin analogy regarding structure and function.

References

BATESON, G., and M. MEAD. *Balinese Character. A Photographic Analysis.* New York: The New York Academy of Sciences, 1942.

BLAUVELT, H. Neonate-mother relationships in goat and man. In *Group*

Processes. Transactions of Second Conference, 1955. Pp. 94–140. New York: Josiah Macy, Jr. Foundation, 1956.

HESS, W. R. *Diencephalon, Autonomic and Extrapyramidal Functions.* New York: Grune & Stratton, Inc., 1954.

HOCKETT, C. Personal communication, 1956.

LORENZ, K. Z. *King Solomon's Ring: New Light on Animal Ways.* New York: Thomas Y. Crowell Company, 1952.

McQUOWN, N. Personal communication, 1956.

SPITZ, R. A. Hospitalism, an inquiry into the genesis of psychiatric conditions in early childhood. In *The Psychoanalytic Study of the Child.* Vol. 1, pp. 53–74. New York: International Universities Press, Inc., 1945.

SPITZ, R. A. Hospitalism, a follow up. In *The Psychoanalytic Study of the Child.* Vol. 2, pp. 113–117. New York: International Universities Press, Inc., 1946.

TINBERGEN, N. *Social Behavior in Animals with Special Reference to Vertebrates.* New York: John Wiley & Sons, Inc., 1953.

TRAGER, G. L. Paralanguage: a first approximation. *Studies in Linguistics, 13:* 1–12 (1958).

TRAGER, G. L., and H. L. SMITH, JR. An outline of English structure. *Studies in Linguistics,* (O. P. 3). Norman, Oklahoma: Battenberg Press, 1951.

WALTER, W. G. *The Living Brain.* New York: W. W. Norton & Company, Inc., 1953.

6

Cultural Problems Posed by a Study of Schizophrenic Process

GREGORY BATESON [1]

The Steady State in Anthropology and Psychiatry

In the years immediately following World War II there occurred a significant change in the whole structuring of theory in the behavioral sciences. These were the years during which cybernetics, the information theory, and the theory of games provided us with entirely new and much more rigorous models for thinking about social and interpersonal processes. The rather crude concepts of *equilibrium* which we had developed before the war were replaced by the more rigorous and more flexible ideas associated with the words *steady state*, which will be used to refer to those equilibria which are maintained by homeostatic mechanisms.

[1] Ethnologist, Veterans Administration Hospital, Palo Alto, California, and Visiting Professor, Department of Anthropology, Stanford University.

The ideas in this lecture represent the combined thinking of the staff of the Project for the Study of Schizophrenic Communication. The staff consists of Gregory Bateson, Jay D. Haley, John H. Weakland, Donald D. Jackson, M.D., and William F. Fry, M.D. The project is financed by the Josiah Macy, Jr. Foundation, administered by the Department of Anthropology at Stanford University, and functions at the Veterans Administration Hospital, Palo Alto, California.

To illustrate this change, fieldwork in a New Guinea community had shown us two processes at work. On the one hand various sorts of symmetrical rivalry among individuals and groups were observed and it was evident that such rivalrous sequences of interaction could be progressive and therefore ultimately pathogenic. If A's rivalrous behavior provokes rivalry in B and vice versa, then unless some corrective phenomenon occurs, the system must go on to disruption. On the other hand, the second process observed involved complementary themes such as dominance-submission, exhibitionism-spectatorship, and succoring-dependence, where the behavior of B fit in with but was not the same as that of A.

It appeared, moreover, that these complementary themes of action were in some sense the psychological opposites of the symmetrical themes. In a symmetrical relationship, if A is ahead of B in some psychological direction, B will respond by trying to catch up, whereas in a complementary relationship, B, if he is already behind, will lag further behind. Or, we may put it this way: in a symmetrical relationship B's strength is a stimulus for A's aggression; whereas in a complementary relationship A's aggression will appear when he sees B's weakness.

This psychological contrast between two themes of human relationship presented the beginnings of a hypothesis which would account for the fact that in a culture where both themes were highly developed, neither theme could progress to such an intensity as to disrupt the system. The hypothesis was that the culture maintained psychological equilibrium by a balancing of these two contrary processes, either of which by itself would lead to disruption. But there was no way of explaining why these two trends should happen to be of equal strength.

When the data were reexamined in terms of steady-state theory, it became evident that the culture does not depend

upon mere coincidence to balance the two contradictory
trends, but that, in fact, an excess of symmetrical behavior
touches off rituals which emphasize complementarity, and
vice versa.

The details of this example have been published elsewhere (1). Here it suffices to present two ideas connected
with the concept *steady state:* (1) that progressive change
in whatever direction must of necessity disrupt the *status
quo;* and (2) that a system may contain homeostatic or feedback loops which will limit or redirect these otherwise disruptive processes.

All steady states, of course, are not desirable nor is all
irreversible change undesirable. And if the discussion so far
has come close to suggesting this, it is because the presentation is deliberately oversimplified by exclusion of the larger
gestalten or contexts, and especially those which involve long
epochs of time. The homeostasis of the New Guinea culture
which has been briefly dissected here may well be such as
to prevent that culture from undergoing adaptive change
under the impact of twentieth-century conditions, and the
steady state which in one sense is so beautifully balanced
may in a wider context contribute to the death of the system.
The norms of a culture may be such that in the long run
that culture cannot live with its neighbors or cannot live
within the wider framework of an embracing industrial
civilization. In such a case we would have to say that the
homeostasis is undesirable in terms of this wider setting.

To illustrate more concretely: in New Guinea the actual
rituals of complementary behavior, which correct for excess
of symmetrical rivalry, involve sexual transvestism. It is
easily conceivable that these rituals might be prohibited by
missionaries or the Occidental government. In such a case,
to obey the government would be to risk internal disruption.

This general theoretical approach seems immediately
applicable to the problems of schizophrenia. What we have

done above is to imagine a culture placed in a double bind. From its own point of view, the culture faces either external extermination or internal disruption, and the dilemma is so constructed as to be a dilemma of *self*-preservation in the most literal sense. Under no circumstances can the preexisting "self" survive. Every move seems to propose either extermination by the larger environment or the pains of inner disruption. Even if the culture elects for external adaptation and by some feat achieves the necessary inner metamorphosis, that which survives will be a different "self."

This brief personification of the cultural system will indicate how it happens that the double-bind paradigm is specifically destructive of self-identification.

The Steady State of the Schizophrenic Family

Following is outlined in formal terms the sort of interaction which we find to be characteristic of the natural history of families which contain schizophrenic or near schizophrenic individuals. First and foremost, that which is characteristic is a very tough stability which Jackson has referred to as *homeostasis* (2). We are not yet in a position to say exactly what variables touch off the corrective processes of this homeostasis, but still the behavior of the system as a whole justifies the use of the word. When the identified patient begins to get well, we observe all sorts of subtle pressure being exerted to perpetuate his illness. However, as is well known, there are many cases in which, as the patient gets well, some other member of the family starts to show symptoms of psychiatric stress. It follows that these families are not simply homeostatic around the invalid status of the particular identified patient. It would seem then that the variables which must at all costs be kept constant are somewhat more abstract or more secret in nature. It is not that at all costs the identified patient must be kept confused;

rather it seems as if the patient himself is an accessory—even a willing sacrifice—to the family homeostasis. If he ceases to play this role, there is a likelihood that some other member of the family will assume it in his place. Like many complex homeostatic systems, the pathogenic family seems to be able, like a newt, to regenerate a missing limb.

This type of phenomenon is of course very familiar in the wider field of group dynamics (3). But its nature and mechanisms are in general obscure except in those cases where definite procedures exist for the regenerative process. We know something of how a committee regenerates a new chairman in place of one who has been lost, but we know virtually nothing of the process which occurs when the same committee loses a member who had inconspicuously performed certain catalytic functions in its meetings. Sometimes "spontaneously" another member who had previously been inactive takes over those functions.

Analogous phenomena also occur in many biological systems. If, for example, the apical shoot of a Christmas tree is cut off, *one* of the first whorl of branches below the cut will bend upward and replace the lost apex. This branch will then lose its former bilateral symmetry and become radially symmetrical like any other apical shoot. Such systems are perhaps best thought of as, in some sense, competitive. The various individuals (in this case, branches) of which the system is composed would seem to be so mutually related that, by their interactions, one will always be selected as the "winner" or as the "loser." This individual then becomes specialized in the functions of this position and in performing these functions actively prevents the other individuals from taking over this specialized role.

The "identified" patient has been mentioned and also the replacement of this individual by another, but it is sometimes not as easy as we politely assume to identify one member of such a family as more specifically sick than the others.

If we define schizophrenia, not in terms of the ability to meet the outside world but more formally in terms of the distortions of communication, then we get a picture of three or four individuals, all with distorted habits of communication but all fitting as differentiated members of a family subculture.[2] This pathogenic subculture is no doubt idiosyncratic or deviant from the subculture of other families in the community, but the problem of homeostasis in this particular family is perhaps not fundamentally different from problems of cultural homeostasis in general.

The members of the pathogenic family are differentiated in their roles and form an interacting and self-maintaining system within which it is scarcely possible to point to one member as causative for the characteristics of the system as a whole. Indeed, the assigning of cause or blame to one or other member of such a plexus presents problems rather similar to those presented by the question "Who is most sick?" The identified patient is most overtly sick, but the family system itself is undoubtedly strange and the strangeness may be specifically located not in the individuals but in the premises governing the differentiation of their roles.

What we observe is homeostatic limitation of change to a narrowly circumscribed region. In fact, in many cases, it looks as if the schizophrenogenic family can only be *stable*, i.e., stay within its restricted limits of change, in the presence of a *reductio ad absurdum* of that philosophy which underlies the role differentiation of the members, and as if this function is supplied by the identified patient.

A philosophy of human relationships which to be viable needs the presence of its own confutation?

The idea is not exactly new. We know, for example, that the philosophy of the police state can be maintained only

[2] For a study of subcultural contrast between families in the normal range see the film "Communication and Interaction in Three Families" by G. Bateson and W. Kees.

in the presence of ostensible criminals and that such a state, if it lacks or cannot detect the real article, will focus attention upon innocent scapegoats. Sometimes even the *myth* of subversive attack may contribute to stabilizing such a philosophic system.

"Prisons are built with the stones of law and brothels with bricks of religion"—and so on. And it is significant that the sociological system—the police state—chosen here to exemplify those philosophies which are stable only in the presence of their own confutation, is in fact a system which promotes paranoid and other schizophrenic symptoms among its members.

It is significant also that this philosophic system, in spite of its ruthlessness, insists upon a superficial benevolence and may even call itself a "Welfare State."

These, however, are only analogies and poetic images. What is needed first from the anthropologists is a general theory of family homeostasis. This will be, no doubt, an abstract theoretical model, deductive from some set of axioms. It will probably owe much to the modern theory of games and perhaps as much to recent developments in the field of genetics and embryology. Already anthropologists and others are beginning to work on this and related problems (4), but it will be several years before they give us much help. For the present we have to concentrate our thinking about family subcultures within the more narrow field of the pathogenic family.

The Family System as Seen by Two Individuals

A composite picture of the interactions in such families, derived from our film recordings of their behavior and our attempts at family therapy, here follows. The schizophrenic communication of the identified patient is appropriate to his perception of what goes on between himself and the other members of the family. He "sees" himself as continually placed in contexts of a certain sort, and it is only fair to say that the context at any given moment is in part determined by his own previous behavior. The other members of the family act and communicate in ways which reinforce the patient's perception and behavior, but they, too, like him, are acting appropriately in the contexts as they perceive them and are themselves contributing by their own previous action to determine the context at any given moment. From the point of view of the patient, the contexts have the following formal structure: a parent whom he intensely both loves and hates emits signals of an incongruent nature. This incongruence is perhaps most clear when one half of the parent's behavior precedes an act of the patient and the other half follows. The parent will, for example, invite the patient to express a courageous opinion, and when that opinion is expressed, will disparage it as unloving, disloyal, disobedient, etc. Characteristically, the first half of the parent's behavior will appear to be set in a certain mode or philosophy of interpersonal relations, while the second half is a denial of this mode and the substitution of another. The first might, for example, be joking (or serious). The patient gives an appropriate response to this mood and finds that the mood has been switched on him. The preliminary smile was only a trap, or the preliminary seriousness was only a trap preceding mockery.

From the patient's point of view his response, sandwiched between these two modalities or logical types, can only be destructive of self. *He* is eliminated in the same sense that the "self" is destroyed in the example given earlier of a culture faced with a double bind. The self which responded seriously to the parental signal must be revised in favor of another self when that serious response is received by the parent as something other than what it was.

If I say something which I intend to be serious and the audience laughs, I may be tempted toward an image of myself as a humorous speaker, but this self-image also may be later destroyed in the same sort of way. If the group here assembled is nonpathogenic, I shall have a chance to settle down to a consistent image of self. If this group is pathogenic, it will never permit this settling down to occur—and I, in turn, will not allow the group to permit it to occur!

There are other features of the context which must also be mentioned. From the point of view of the identified patient, there is, or appears to be, an absolute prohibition upon calling attention to the parent's incongruity in any overt way. It was said that the patient "sees" himself as in a bind, but this must now be qualified to say that the prohibition upon comment may be so strong as to result in something like a repression of his perception of the bind. Neither the parent nor the patient is able to act as if fully aware of the incongruities.

There is also a prohibition upon escaping from the field, and, in addition, an insistence on the part of the parent that the patient respond. There shall be no nonresponding and no not caring. And all these prohibitions are linked together. After all, to leave the field or to express "not caring" would be to point a finger at the incongruities.

The Typical Schizophrenic Message

Under these circumstances, the human being will appropriately protect himself by emitting messages which cannot be maltreated. Characteristically, this is done by stripping the message of all explicit or implicit metacommunicative material. For instance, if you look at a Western Union telegraph blank, you will see that it has a space for the text of the message and a number of other spaces for material which will label this text, classifying the message under such categories as to whom, from whom, date, place, time, priority,

codes used, and so forth. All this latter material—the procedural part of his message—the schizophrenic will omit or
distort. In addition, he will distort the text itself at precisely
those points where procedural or metacommunicative inferences might be drawn. For example, pronouns will be
avoided, and similarly he will avoid all indications of what
sort of relationship might obtain between himself and the
person he is addressing. He will falsify the priorities of his
utterance, indicating a high importance for a relatively
trivial message or denying the importance of a message which
he feels to be vital. In addition, he may code the message
in a metaphoric form without indicating that such a code
is being used. Even a second metaphoric code may be superposed upon the first. Lastly, the message, so distorted, may
be made to simulate an objective message about some other
subject in the real world. The schizophrenic may even make
very small changes in a straightforward mesage, changes just
sufficient to enable him to tell himself secretly that this is
not *his* message. He may, for example, call himself W. Edward Jones, when his real name is Edward W. Jones—like a
child who crosses his fingers behind his back while telling
a fib.

But the identified schizophrenic may engage in attack as
well as defense. He may attempt to turn the tables upon the
parent, either by responding as though the parent's initial
message were of some sort different from what the parent
intended, or he may seek to impose upon the parent those
prohibitions which surround the double bind—the prohibition on commenting upon incongruity or the prohibition on
withdrawing from the field—or he may attempt to insist upon
response.

All of this, both attack and defense, is sane behavior in
the sense of being understandable under the circumstances as
defined—by the schizophrenic subject. The boundary of
sanity is, however, crossed when the subject uses these tricks

of communication in situations which the common man—one hesitates to say the "normal"—would not perceive as the schizophrenic seems to perceive them.

This discussion is not meant to digress into an elaborate discussion of learning theory (5). It is limited to asserting that recurrent experience of reinforcing contexts, which, though they may vary in content have again and again the same formal pattern, will result in a learning to expect this formal pattern. The individual with such experience will expect the repetition of such patterns and will even act as though such patterns surrounded him. And he will do this even when the indications for the existence of these patterns are minimal or would be subliminal for other persons with a different history. For example, the whole theory of transference in Freudian psychoanalysis depends upon this or some similar assumption. The patient is seen as responding to the analyst as though the latter were behaving in ways in which the patient perhaps unconsciously believes that his parent behaved. In other words, he responds in the presence of the analyst as if the latter's communication provided patterned contexts similar to those in which he learned his eating, walking, sphincter control, and the like.

In terms of this premise from learning theory, it becomes expectable that the individual subjected to repeated double-bind traumata will act as though this traumatic context continually surrounds him, even at times when more normal individuals would regard such behavior as "crazy."

So much for the identified overtly schizophrenic member of the family whom I have pictured as vis-à-vis a "parent." Actually, he must in general deal with two parents, and I shall now describe the family system from their points of view.

One of the patients with whom we have worked extensively sent to his mother on Mother's Day a commercially printed card which said "For someone who has been like a mother to me." In so doing, he was of course putting her in a double bind. From her point of view, any future spontaneous maternal behavior on her part was threatened with being relabeled and perhaps mislabeled as some sort of theatrical display and hypocrisy not coming from the heart. However much the son's jibe may have been deserved, it was still a threat to the mother's "self." She immediately came to the hospital with the card in her hand "to know what he meant." With extreme courage the son managed to say that he had meant "to sting her a little," but this reply she could not accept; she had to force him to complete confusion and a verbal agreement that it was "all a mistake." [3]

This incident illustrates one of the most destructive forms of double bind, namely the attack upon spontaneity or sincerity. This is overtly used by the parent when the identified patient does something which might seem to be generous or kind. "You only did it to please me. You didn't really *mean* it" or even "you only did it because I asked you to." And conversely, every therapist who has dealt with the overtly psychotic person is familiar with the patient's suspicious attack (often covert) upon his therapist's motives and spontaneity. Characteristically this species of double bind sets the inner process of the mind or heart against the outward overt behavior, and the victim is placed in precisely the position which I envisaged for the New Guinea culture: either the inner man must be sacrificed or the outer behavior will court destruction.

In fact, the double-binding interaction is a sort of battle around the question of whose self shall be destroyed. And a basic characteristic of the family, which is shared by all the relevant members, is the premise that the self is destroyed or can be destroyed in this battle—and *therefore* the

[3] Compare Jay D. Haley, "The Family of the Schizophrenic." To be published.

fight must go on.[4] "Tweedledum and Tweedledee *agreed* to have a battle."

But in the families which we have studied we find almost universally implicit agreement on the part of the parents to deny that any such battle exists. And the identified patient, though he may know about the battle, dares not remark upon it. The family, after all, is not an isolated entity. It is a part of the larger community and has all sorts of contacts outside, and the "sane" members of the family are always anxious about these. One patient neatly expressed the matter when I asked him what he thought his mother was most afraid of. He replied "the aperiential securities," neatly telescoping into a single neologism both her fear of outward loss of prestige vis-à-vis the neighbors should she cease to maintain physiologic control, and her inner fear of what her bowels might do if she should succeed in controlling them.

The role of the father seems in general to be less heroic than that of either the patient or the mother. And indeed one's first impulse when confronted with such a family is to try to give the father a shot in the arm which will enable him to stand up and challenge the basic hypocrisy and cruelty with which he is surrounded. Perhaps this impulse is appropriate. I do not know as yet.

Be that as it may, the father, as he is, acts as another factor in maintaining the family homeostasis within its restricted range. His behavior vis-à-vis the identified patient may range from giving his passive consent to the operations of the mother—which operations she commonly practices also upon him—to an active participation in constructing traumatic contexts for the patient. He may join in the insistence that the patient shall not escape from the field and in

[4] For a mathematical analysis of the conditions for homeostatic balance in armaments races, see, for example: L. F. Richardson. "Generalized foreign politics," *British Journal of Psychology Monograph Supplement.* No. 23, 1939.

the insistence that the patient respond. He may actively tease the patient, thereby further reducing the latter's self-confidence; and it is probable (though here our data are poor) that the father may contribute to the double binds by remarks which are contrapuntal to the messages of the mother, so that the identified patient is sometimes sand-wiched not between two utterances of the mother, but between an utterance of hers and another coming from the father.

In one instance, the mother scolded her 16-year-old psy-chotic son for calling his 3-year-old younger sister a "boy." The father joined her in forbidding this, and she turned on him and told him to shut up—*she* would handle it. If the boy obeyed his father even when the father was only repeat-ing what the mother had said, he would be going against his mother's wishes.

As regards the related matter of conflict between mother and father, the findings are clear: *covert* conflict tends to increase the psychotic symptoms of the identified patient, whereas the change from covert to overt conflict tends to diminish these symptoms. And the same generalization seems to apply to authority figures *in loco parentis,* such as the doctor and the nurse (6).

No doubt the concealment of the conflict constitutes a message to the identified patient: probably a command that he shall not comment upon the disagreement. This may be sufficient to evoke from him that behavior which he has learned to exhibit in those double-bind contexts. But the matter is not clear and the concealment of the parental con-flict might equally be, to that offspring, a destructive de-mand for self-control. Interestingly enough in the Balinese ritual drama, trance behavior is evoked in the young men by *overt* conflict between Witch and Dragon, the parental protagonists (7).

The Cultural Problems

The following summary of the clinical picture of the family is an effort to bring out some of the questions which anthropologists might answer. What has here been sketched is unfortunately not a theory of schizophrenia, nor even a theory of the communicational aspects of that pathology. Rather, it is a *family* of such theories. From what has been said, one could construct a vast range of different communicational models, any one of which would be possibly schizophrenogenic. I have not attempted to select one of these alternatives, nor have I even attempted any classification within the family of possible explanatory models. For example, too great a focus on the mother in the pathogenic family has been avoided because there is no a priori reason within the theory which would lead us to expect this relative to have special significance. It is true, of course, that she has special functions in the prenatal and infantile period of life. But this circumstance is, in a sense, irrelevant or accidental to the formal cybernetic model. The entities or individuals composing such a model are not human, and schizophrenogenic models could therefore be set up in which the role assigned to the mother could be assigned to any other member of the intimate unit, or—and this is the more interesting case—this role could be unlocalized. The family unit as a whole could behave *as if* it contained a member whose role would be that assigned here to the pathogenic mother; but it conceivably might contain no such member. The pathogenic nature of the family unit might result only from its characteristics as an organizational network. If we see an engine behaving as if it contained a governor, we are not entitled from this external characteristic of the engine to say that in fact there is a *localized* governor inside the system. The self-corrective characteristic of the system may result from the total network structure.

To summarize, then, what can be said about the family of theories offered here, what are the common characteristics of all members of this family of theories?

1. The theories assume three levels or systems of gestalten: A, B, and C, so related that A is a part of B, and B is a part of C.

2. In this system of wheels within wheels, the A's are entities capable of internal homeostasis, complex learning, and complex external communication with each other. They are the analogues of human individuals.

3. The gestalt called B is composed of several A's. It is the analogue of the family. This unit also is characterized by internal homeostasis and probably certain sorts of primitive learning.

4. The largest gestalt, C, is the analogue of the community. It is composed of many B's. This, too, is a homeostatic unit, complexly organized, and susceptible of changes which are the sociological analogues of learning.

5. The theories of pathogenic process suggest that these three homeostatic gestalten may be interrelated in the following way: The A's, or individuals, contain processes of the "positive feedback" or "regenerative" type, i.e., processes which, if uncontrolled, would lead to unlimited directional change and therefore to the destruction of the A system as such. These regenerative processes are, however, limited by superposed homeostatic controls. (It will be noted that these statements about the internal functioning of the individuals are beyond the scope of psychological or anthropological investigation. We can only see and hear the external communication of the individual. Inside the "black box" is physiology.)

6. The unit B is so constructed that its stability depends upon some process in a direction which precludes or is pre-

cluded by the homeostatic processes within the individuals. The family can be stable only if the individual relaxes that internal control upon which his personal stability depends.

7. Similarly, the stability of B within the larger community unit C depends upon homeostatic processes which preclude those upon which the stability of B depends.

Our prediction amounts to this: in any such total system, the units at the B level, the families, will have the characteristics which we have called *schizophrenogenic*. That is, the identity of the component individuals will be blurred in their communications with each other, and every component individual will be under some pressure pushing him or her toward that *reductio ad absurdum* of the blurring of identity which we call *schizophrenia*.

Lastly, the stability of the family unit will be enhanced if one member of the family takes this path toward the *reductio ad absurdum*.

With this generalized picture, let me now turn to my colleagues in anthropology and present them with some questions:

1. Anthropology has devoted a great deal of work since the publication of Ruth Benedict's *Patterns of Culture* to showing how character formation operates in different cultures. In the main, they have shown that the patterns of child raising and the family configuration within which the child is a member are congruent with the patterns of adult life in the various areas of religion, mythology, warfare, technology, art, etc. But the accent has been put upon answering always the positive question, "How are the babies in the given culture made into characteristic members of that culture?" Now here is the converse question "How are the babies prevented from becoming exaggerated versions—caricatures—of the cultural norm?" We know that in some cultures such exaggerations of particular cultural patterns occur sporadically from time to time. What failures of what

preventive process lead to these sporadic exaggerations? And how is their more frequent occurrence prevented?

2. The first question is really the paradigm for the others. What we need in order to construct a generalized theory of the family (within which the pathogenic family will be a special case) is a mapping of the homeostatic mechanisms which determine family organizations. How are the three homeostatic systems listed above—the individual, the family, and the community—interrelated so as to avoid the conflicts of homeostasis which are here proposed as pathogenic? The anthropologists have given one half of an answer to questions about homeostasis. They collect the data which will demonstrate that learning, or character formation, or organizational differentiation proceed in some given direction. But they do not also ask the converse question: "What are the upper limits of process in this direction?" Is the process limited by some corrective feedback? And what variables activate this feedback? What "symptoms" in individual behavior or subgroup characteristics serve to evoke the corrective process?

3. And apart from these general questions about homeostasis in human communities, what has been said about schizophrenia poses a number of more specific questions. It is not much use to ask the anthropologist to bring us statistics about the incidence of schizophrenia in different cultures, until the disease has been defined in some way which will be cross-culturally acceptable. We can, however, ask questions about the sorts of family pathology that occur in the particular cultures which anthropologists study. I have mentioned earlier the very conspicuous differences in family subculture which occur among the middle-class families in urban northern California. We need similar studies of family subcultures in the supposedly more homogenous preliterate communities. Work of this kind is a necessary preliminary to a study of the pathologies of family homeostasis in different cultural settings. Only after this can we meaningfully

ask about the specific roles of father, mother, spouse, grand-parents, and so forth, in the pathogenic families in the particular culture.

To conclude on a more positive note, what has been said here has exposed vast areas about which we know almost nothing. But it is a great advance that we can now ask questions of the sort which I have tried to raise. We have in our hands the conceptual tools which enable us to pose the questions, and we have had these tools for less than twenty years. We are only just beginning the exciting task of exploring their potentialities.

Discussion

Robert A. Kimmich [5]

Mr. Bateson has stimulated us by a number of fascinating formulations and observations relating to the schizophrenic and his family, but at the same time has frustrated us by many brief allusions to the wealth of his background material with which many of us are unfamiliar.

This work was purposely prepared to raise questions rather than to answer them, and some very cogent ones have been asked. One of these major questions relates to why some people do *not* become psychotic in spite of severe stress. It seems that the study of health has always been more difficult than investigation of illness. Another question was posed early in the paper in regard to a balancing of two potentially disruptive processes: namely, direct rivalry and complementary behavior. The core problem for investigation here seems to be the matter of the linkage between the two poles of this self-balancing system.

A very interesting concept presented by Mr. Bateson is that of so-called *family homeostasis*, as coined by Jackson.

[5] Chief, Professional Education, Stockton State Hospital, Stockton, California; formerly, Medical Director, Territorial Hospital, Kaneohe, Hawaii.

In this we are shown a characteristic observed by the author in the families of schizophrenics. The terms *stability, homeostasis,* and *steady state* seem to be used more or less interchangeably. This refers to an *excessive* stability in the organization and functioning of a family subculture. This type of stability appears to be similar to the rigidity of individual character structure and also rigid family behavior noted in other studies of neurosis and prepsychosis. By this analogy, one may be further helped to see the potential brittleness of such an adaptive pattern in a family group. In this case the brittleness is not that of an all-or-none type but rather one which forces dynamic redefinition of roles within the family setting.

In this concept Mr. Bateson has suggested a provocative, different view of social pathology in the family of a schizophrenic by stressing the dynamic *self-perpetuation* of the pathologically stable system. It is easily inferred that such a type and degree of stability is antithetical to adaptability.

Distorted and inadequate communication is mentioned as being just as characteristic of the total family behavior as for the identified schizophrenic patient within it. Thus even in prepsychotic years, distorted communication is a way of life. The strange behavior and verbalizations of the schizophrenic are probably not only appropriate to his perceptions but also are disguised attempts to communicate and relate with others.

The author has well described for us the conflict situation in which the schizophrenic finds himself. Basically, he is neither able to be independently aggressive nor is he able to be passively conforming. The first action would lead to destruction from without, but the second would lead to sacrifice of the self. He can neither fight nor fly with success.

It is unlikely that this particular conflict configuration is specific for schizophrenia alone, although it is clearly observed with these patients. I doubt if Mr. Bateson intended such an implication since his questions at the end of the paper indicated awareness that the type of social conflict is probably not enough to explain development of a specific symptom picture.

Mr. Bateson's observations indicate that such a family has usually developed a social system which uses and perpetuates contradictory attitudes but does not allow opportunity for solution of resultant conflicts. This is partly due to prohibition of overt expression of attitudes deviant from the family conformity pattern. This avoidance of direct discussion of feelings and the realities of life has also been noted by others in this same context.

Our work here with various ethnic groups tends to agree with some of the observations made in this paper. For example, the second and third generation child of Japanese immigrant ancestry shows a high tendency to become schizophrenic if he becomes psychotic. The psychosocial conflict between conformity to parental ways and rebelling against them is prominent and rather easily studied here. Development of a clear self-concept has been almost impossible for many of these people when they find themselves, in the *family* setting, caught between East and West.

I, too, hope that much work will be done in these areas outlined by Mr. Bateson; but, I also feel it would be unfair to ask the anthropologists to do it all.

References

1a. BATESON, GREGORY. *Naven*. London: Cambridge University Press, 1936.
 b. BATESON, GREGORY. *Epilogue 1958*. (2d ed. of *Naven*). Stanford: Stanford University Press, 1958.
2. JACKSON, DONALD D. The question of family homeostasis. *Psychoanal. Quart.*, Supplement, *31*: 79–90 (1957).
3. REDL, FRITZ. *4th Conference on Group Processes*. Josiah Macy, Jr. Foundation (to be published). The regenerative characteristics of groups of children are here discussed in detail, and analogous examples are drawn from the field of animal behavior, including organizations of ants and bees.

4a. BAVELAS, ALEX. *Group Processes Conference, 1957*. New York: Josiah Macy, Jr. Foundation.

 b. ROMNEY, KIM. "Structural Analysis of Cross-cousin Marriage." Ph.D. dissertation, Harvard University, 1956.

 c. VON NEUMANN, J., and O. MORGENSTERN. *Theory of Games and Economic Behavior*. Rev. ed. Princeton, N. J.: Princeton University Press, 1955.

 d. WADDINGTON, C. H. *Strategy of the Genes*. London: George Allen & Unwin, Ltd., 1957.

5a. BATESON, G. Social planning and the concept of "deutero-learning." *Conference on Science, Philosophy, and Religion, Second Symposium*. New York: Harper & Brothers, 1942.

 b. HARLOW, H. F. The formation of learning sets. *Psychol. Rev. 56:* 51–65 (1949).

 c. RUESCH, J., and G. BATESON. *Communication: The Social Matrix of Psychiatry*. New York: W. W. Norton & Company, Inc., 1951.

6. STANTON, A. H., and M. S. SCHWARTZ. *The Mental Hospital*. New York: Basic Books, Inc., 1954.

7. BATESON, G., and M. MEAD. *Balinese Character. A Photographic Analysis*. The New York Academy of Sciences, 1942.

7

Family Relationships in Schizophrenia

MURRAY BOWEN [1]

Two hundred years ago, Laurence Sterne (1), in his novel *The Life and Opinions of Tristram Shandy* described family relationships in a way that is strikingly appropriate today. Tristram Shandy said, "Though in one sense, our family was certainly a simple machine, as it consisted of a few wheels, yet there was this much to be said for it, that these wheels were set in motion by so many different springs, and acted one upon the other from such a variety of strange principles and impulses—that though it was a simple machine, it had all the honor and advantages of a complex one—and a number of as odd movements within it, as ever were beheld in the inside of a Dutch silkmill."

In this paper some relationship patterns observed in families with a schizophrenic son or daughter are to be described. The families have been part of a clinical research project in which fathers, mothers, schizophrenic patients, and normal siblings have lived together on a psychiatric ward in a research center. Four of these in-residence families have now participated in the research study and in family psycho-

[1] Chief, Family Study Section, Clinical Investigations, National Institute of Mental Health, Bethesda, Maryland.

therapy for periods up to 2½ years. The average length of in-residence participation has been 1½ years. An additional six families consisting of fathers, mothers, and moderately disturbed psychotic patients have been treated in outpatient family psychotherapy for periods up to 2 years. The study is an intensive longitudinal one which has followed the clinical course of ten family groups for fairly long periods of time. The most important part of the research study has been the four in-residence families. The parents assume the major responsibility for the psychotic family member. The structure permits a parent to work and the normal sibling to attend school, but it requires the family to attend the daily family psychotherapy hours. There are detailed around-the-clock observations on each family member. This longitudinal view of the families, as they live, eat, play, and work together through periods of success, failure, crisis, and physical illness provides our best source of subjective and objective research data.

The theoretical orientation and the psychotherapy approach for this project was developed from experience during the first year of the project. During that year three schizophrenic patients and their mothers lived together on the ward. Each patient and each mother had individual psychotherapy. The details of that part of the study have been reported in other papers (2, 3, 4). To summarize briefly, there had been increasing experience to suggest that the mother-patient relationship was a dependent fragment of a larger family problem and that the father played an important part in it. The research hypothesis was extended to consider the psychosis in the patient as the symptom manifestation of a problem that involved the entire family. The research plan was changed to permit entire family groups to live on the ward together. The psychotherapy plan was changed to make it more consistent with the research hypothesis. The new plan was one in which family members attended all psychotherapy hours together. We [2] have called this *family psychotherapy*. There are two important concepts in this theoretical orientation. The first is the concept of the family unit. We attempt to think of the family and to relate to the family as though it were a single unit or single organism. The second is the concept of family psychotherapy. We attempt to direct the psychotherapy to the family unit rather than to the individual.

A major problem has been the orientation of ourselves to a family-unit way of thinking. We have all been trained to think of emotional problems in terms of the individual. The entire body of psychoanalytic and psychological theory is oriented to the individual. All our diagnostic and descriptive terms apply to the individual. It has been difficult to change this automatic way of thinking in ourselves. Even after the staff had achieved some success at thinking of the family as a unit, we found that the use of familiar psychiatric terms could result in an immediate associative shift back to "second-nature" individual orientation. To facilitate the shift to family-unit thinking, we have tried to avoid the use of terms associated with the individual and to force ourselves to use simple descriptive words. Another difficulty in the family-unit orientation is an emotional one. In our daily living experience, we all constantly participate emotionally in the life about us. We identify ourselves with the victim, we applaud the hero, and we hate the villain. A family in daily living contact with a psychotic member has a high level of anxiety and emotion. There are frequent emotional crises that portray one member as victim, another as hero, and another as villain. It is easy for the observer to become so

[2] "We" refers to the staff of the research project. This includes the author, Robert H. Dysinger, M.D., Warren M. Brodey, M.D., and Betty Basamania, M.S.S. In this paper the words "we" or "our" will be used to refer to ideas generally accepted by the staff and included in the operating policy of the project. "I" and "my" will refer to points in my thinking that are not part of the operating policy of the project.

involved in the emotion that he loses objectivity. The emotional situation is further complicated by the efforts of each family member to find a staff ally for his or her emotional point of view. Staff members have tended to detach themselves emotionally to the point that they can work with the families without becoming overinvolved in the vigorous ebb and flow of conflictual emotion.

We believe there are certain distinct advantages to having a family-unit orientation in addition to our more familiar individual orientation. When it is possible to defocus the individual, to find a perspective that permits the entire family into vision at once, and to continue the observations for long periods, it is then possible to get a much clearer view of over-all patterns. We have compared this to changing the lens of a microscope from the oil-immersion to a low-power lens, or to moving from the playing field to the top of the stadium to watch a football game. The view from the top of the stadium makes it possible to see broad patterns of movement and team functioning that are obscured by the close-up view. It is easier to see the team as a unit from this perspective. This in no way detracts from the value of the individual orientation. In fact, the distant view enhances the close-up view. For instance, the high magnification of the oil-immersion lens is far more meaningful after it has been possible to see the larger area through the low-power lens. The broader viewpoint, maintained over long periods of time, helps to put clinical fragments into place. For example, we often hear statements like, "The father was seductive toward the daughter." In our experience with these families, this might be descriptively accurate in describing an occasional or transient phase in their relationship but inaccurate and misleading if applied to their over-all relationship. We agree with those who would like to have a family diagnosis in addition to individual diagnoses. Ackerman (5) has worked toward defining interlocking pathology in family relationships. Mittelman (6) has described reciprocal relationships between family members. After working at this problem for over three years, our effort has been going toward some kind of concept that deals with the *function* of one person in relation to another, rather than with the more static situation implied in a diagnostic label. Spiegel (7) includes the idea of function in his work on role theory, though it is not specifically stressed.

In this paper I wish to focus on the *functioning* of one person in relation to another and on broad *patterns* of behavior that are more easily seen from "the top of the stadium." I shall defocus, as much as possible, the more specific relationship characteristics which have been reported in other papers. In this regard, our observations of specific characteristics have much in common with the work of Lidz and Fleck (8, 9), Jackson and Bateson (10), and Wynne (11). The main part of this paper will be devoted to the clinical course of a single family. Before considering the single family, however, some of the over-all *patterns* of family *functioning* that appear to us to be most important are here reviewed. These patterns of functioning have been presented in more detail in other papers (4, 12), but they are of sufficient importance to the understanding of this presentation to be reviewed here.

There has been a high level of emotional conflict in the research families. For brief periods the conflict may be equally present in several family members. The conflict tends to localize in the family member who is in the weakest and most inadequate position. The localization occurs through a process of reciprocal functioning in which all family members participate. The conflict tends to localize in the schizophrenic member. When the emotional conflict is "fixed" in the weakest member by means of a diagnosis and by the designation of *patient*, the family problem becomes more crystalized in the person of the patient, and anxiety in the family is greatly decreased. When the parents and patients are brought together in a living situation in a hospital ward, and the designation *patient* is purposely left ambiguous, the family conflict again becomes more fluid and shifting. Parents begin to develop intense anxiety and conflict. Such a family can accurately be called a *disturbed family*.

Family members, and especially the parents, are quite different in their business and social relationships outside the family from what they are to those within the family. The parents might function adequately and successfully in outside business and social relationships while they are immature, indecisive, and inadequate within the family. The primary family members involved in the family conflict are the father, mother, and the patient. Other family members are involved to a much lesser extent. This was particularly striking in the families in which normal siblings lived in residence as long as one year. There were times when the normal siblings were intensely involved, but they could always separate themselves from the conflict and leave the father, mother, and patient to continue in cyclical conflict. We have referred to the father, mother, and patient as the *interdependent triad*.

There is a striking emotional distance between the parents in all the families. We have called this the *emotional divorce*. As I see it, the situation began early in the marriage with alternating periods of overcloseness and overdistance which then settled down to the more fixed, and less anxious, emotional distance. Some parents maintain the distance with a very formal, positive, and controlled relationship. These marriages have the words and actions to give a superficial appearance of closeness, but feeling and emotion is obliterated from the parental relationships. Other parents have so much emotion and disagreement that they use physical distance to maintain the "divorce." Most parents use combinations of controlled positiveness and physical distance.

The parents in all the families have a constant pattern of functioning in their relationship together. We have called this the *overadequate-inadequate reciprocity*. Both parents are equally immature. In any teamwork activity, the one who makes decisions for the two of them becomes the overadequate one and the other becomes the inadequate or helpless one. Neither is able to find mid-ground functioning between the two extremes. The overadequate one is seen as dominating, authoritative, or stubborn and the inadequate one as helpless, compliant, and forced into submission by the dominant one. Either mother or father can function in either position though they eventually find an equilibrium in which one is overadequate in most areas and the other overadequate in fewer areas. They tend to solve the anxiety of the overadequate-inadequate reciprocity in rather consistent ways. They can reduce the areas of joint activity and increase their individual activities. It is common for fathers to devote themselves almost entirely to business and for mothers to be completely in charge of home and children. When they do encounter a decision in the area of joint activity, they have either to avoid the decision, postpone it, or face the anxiety and conflict when one "takes the bull by the horns" and assumes the overadequate position. An example is a father who has no problem in important decisions at work but who can end up in an emotional, paralyzing deadlock when he and the mother try to decide which movie to see.

All the parents have highly charged opposing viewpoints about how to relate to the psychotic patient. This seems to be their one joint activity about which conflict remains most intense. They do not reveal such conflict about the normal siblings. The parents may not become aware of the disagreement about the patient until psychotherapy is under way. A familiar pattern is one in which the mother had her way while the father retreated and said nothing about his intense opposing viewpoint. The mother may go many years believing the father to be in agreement with her viewpoint and then be completely surprised to hear of his long-term opposition. If the parents disagree openly, they may alternate their plans for the patient, each one "letting the other have his way to prove him wrong."

There are some constant relationship patterns within the interdependent triad. The parents are separated from each other by the emotional divorce. They cannot have a close relationship with each other, but either can have a close relationship with the patient if the other permits. Functionally, this is similar to the way divorced parents share their children. The mother usually has the primary relationship or "custody" of the patient while the father is excluded or permits himself to be excluded from the intense mother-patient relationship. There are repeating situations that follow the same pattern. The mother does things to keep the patient attached to her. Verbally, she blames the father for his lack of interest in the patient. The father has actually been making a long-term effort to win the patient to his side. He sees his poor relationship with the patient as his failure to be a good father. When the mother accuses him of neglecting the patient, he tries to get close to the patient. If the patient shows too much interest in the father, the mother moves to intensify the patient's attachment to her. There are several variations to the pattern. Mothers arrange for fathers and patients to spend regular time together, but they initiate it and the father in such a case functions more like a baby sitter than a father. The psychotic patient can become so hostile and aggressive that the mother rejects the patient or goes away. The father then moves into what would appear to be a close relationship, but, in our experience, the father still functions as a substitute mother and the mother can usually win back the patient, even after long absences. As I currently see it, the father has somehow to deal directly with the mother before he can have a real father relationship to the patient.

Now to a consideration of family psychotherapy and to some of the sharp, clear changes in family functioning that have occurred during the course of family psychotherapy. These changes have been of crucial importance in the research study. The first such change came unexpectedly some six months after the first family was admitted. The father had slowly changed from a passive compliant fellow to a man of more strength and conviction. When he had reached a point of self-assertion that was greater than the mother's aggression and domination, she immediately went through a series of dramatic changes. She had long been the resourceful and overadequate one in the family. Within a few days she became tremulous, tearful, and overtly anxious. She was fearful and felt helpless. The father maintained his stand in spite of her anxiety and within two weeks she had changed to a calm, objective, firm, motherly person. She said, "If he can keep on being a man, then I can be a woman." The emotional divorce was resolved and the father and mother were as devoted to each other as a teen-age couple in love for the first time. They were so much invested in each other that neither was overinvested in the patient. Both were then able, for the first time, to be objective toward the patient. At this point, the schizophrenic daughter began some significant changes toward more adequate functioning. The new functioning level lasted a month and then the family suddenly reverted to the old way of functioning; but thereafter, it was easier for the father to pull up to more adequate functioning and less threatening for the mother to give up the overadequate position. It was this change and similar changes in other families that highlighted facets of the problem not particularly noted before. It was the changes in the families during family psychotherapy that led to the concept of the functioning of one person in relation to another. Before this experience, we had thought in terms of "the father *is* one kind of person, the mother *is* another kind of person, and the patient *becomes* another kind of person." The research operation had first gone toward defining what we believed to be the fixed characteristics of each family member. After we had seen changes in one family member followed by immediate complementing changes in other family members, and after we had seen changes in characteristics formerly considered to be fixed, we began to work toward the concept of the functioning of one person in relation to another.

The techniques of the family psychotherapy were developed from clinical observation in the research study. After a clinical pattern had repeated itself sufficiently to permit an extension in theoretical thinking, the working hypothesis was extended. Then the psychotherapy approach was changed to make it as consistent as possible with the research hypothesis. In this way the theoretical thinking and the psychotherapy complemented each other. We have attempted to differentiate family psychotherapy from individual and from group psychotherapy. Individual psychotherapy focuses on psychological understanding of the individual in terms of concepts developed for the individual. The analysis of the transference relationship between patient and therapist is an important part of the treatment process. One of our goals in family psychotherapy is to leave the already existing intense relationships within the family group and to analyze the relationships *in situ* rather than to permit transfer to the relationship with the therapist. An effort has been made to define and to avoid those things which encourage the individual relationship with the resulting transference to the therapist. We believe it is technically possible for the analyst to remain in a fairly objective relationship to the family organism in this way. Of course, the analyst hopefully remains objective when he is in an individual relationship with a psychotic patient, but the patient has the potential of creating a crisis which can force the analyst into dealing with, rather than analyzing the crisis situation. In family psychotherapy, the parents are present to deal with the upset in the patient and the therapist is free to remain an observer and to analyze the situation in which one side of the family organism acts up against the other side. It should be obvious that the therapist is not permitted to participate in the intense emotional process in the family. Even when the therapist takes sides without expressing it, the other family members can become aware of it and react negatively toward this countertransference participation. When the therapist can avoid individual relationships, there usually develops a dependent relationship with the family unit which is then analyzed.

Family psychotherapy is also clearly differentiated from group psychotherapy. A psychotherapy group is an assembly of people brought together with a therapeutic goal. Group members are comparative strangers in contrast to the intense interdependent relationships between family members. A goal of group therapy is to understand the individual in the context of his relationships in a group of other individuals.

The clinical course of a single family in outpatient psychotherapy with a single therapist will be used to illustrate the changes in family functioning during psychotherapy and to illustrate the principles of family psychotherapy as developed in the research project. A single therapist with a single family is the simplest example of our psychotherapy effort. The inpatient families become involved in complex relationships with the staff, other family groups, and with the hospital environment. As a group the outpatient families have progressed more rapidly in family therapy.

The family to be described is one that has progressed most rapidly and that has shown striking changes in relationship functioning. The family history is very similar to that of several families in the study. The parents were in their fifties. The psychotic patient was a daughter in her late twenties who had been overtly psychotic for six years. The father was a quiet, soft-spoken businessman who had devoted most of his energies to his business. He often worked nights and weekends. At home he functioned as the provider and the one responsible for repairs and maintenance of the home. All his life he had worried about financial security. The mother was an outgoing, aggressive, resourceful woman who managed to keep going even when she did not feel like it. During their thirty years of marriage, the mother had devoted herself to the children and the home while the father had devoted himself to the business. Within the family the mother was the overadequate decision-making one while the father remained on the periphery of the family circle. The daughter had been the helpless inadequate one since her first acute psychotic break while still in college. She was the oldest of two daughters. The other daughter, three years younger, had been relatively uninvolved in the family turmoil. She separated herself from the family after college and has made a good adjustment.

The family was prominent and respected in the small town in which they lived. The father had moved to this town as a single man to establish his business. He met the mother through a business acquaintance when she visited the town. They had a brief courtship. He took a few days from his business for the wedding. The business did well. After a few years they built a new home in one of the better sections of town. This house is still the family home. The family group consisted of father, mother, and the two daughters. The mother wanted children for "my fulfillment as a woman." The father wanted to wait until their financial future was more secure. The mother was overinvested in the child by the time she knew she was pregnant. Her overinvestment was expressed in fears, concerns, and worries that the child would be defective or born dead. Her worries about the child were more intense when she was emotionally detached from the father. The worries decreased when she was closer to the father. She felt a great relief when she first saw the baby and could see for herself that it was alive and well. She was impressed by the "tiny helplessness" of the baby. She felt a surge of maternal instinct to protect and care for the child. The second daughter never occupied this position of importance in the mother's thoughts.

The mother's overinvestment in the first daughter continued over the years. When the second child was born, she was impressed with the reaction of the older child and decided, "she needs me more than the baby." Through the years she worried about the daughter's development, her appearance, her dress, her hair, her complexion, her social life, and many other such items. There was much less concern about the second daughter who, "somehow was able to get along by herself." In childhood the daughter was shy, immature, and compliant. She was bright and she learned quickly but she was very attached to the mother and "she never learned how to relate with other children." The father and mother had become increasingly distant in their relationship. He was completely involved with the business while the mother was devoted to doing a good job with the children. She felt there was no sacrifice too great for the children, especially the older daughter, who seemed to need so much more from the mother. Socially the parents were congenial. Their social relationships were not close but they belonged to social and civic clubs and they were active in their home town. At home they had sharp differences in opinion and frequent arguments, but they avoided touchy points to keep disagreements at a minimum.

There were several changes in the family during a two-year period when the daughter reached adolescence. The daughter was much attached to the mother. She began to act very grown-up and to deny the need for the mother. She had been shy and inhibited in her school relationships. Now she became outgoing, overactive, and pushed in her drive for friends.

The mother was offered a job and she began to work. The father had some business reverses, but he took on additional business responsibility and began to work longer hours. The parents moved to separate bedrooms at home. The family kept up this increased tempo of living for several years. The daughter was vaguely aware of her dependence on the mother, but she looked forward to college and living away from home to bring about an emancipation from the family.

The daughter developed her first acute psychotic break while living away at college. This was the beginning of a six-year period of psychosis and family prostration. The psychotic daughter was hospitalized and for the next several years she was either acutely psychotic and in a hospital or living at home on a borderline adjustment. The mother pulled up to her most overadequate level of functioning. She assumed responsibility for the daughter and made the decisions for hospitalization against the daughter's protests. The father had a series of business reverses and within a year after the psychosis in the daughter, he lost his business. The mother was the decision-making breadwinner for the family. Her thoughts were almost totally invested in the daughter. The father worked at a number of different jobs, but he was at the most ineffective period in his life. He was opposed to the mother's decisions about the daughter but, on the surface, he went along with her. The only one who changed during this period was the younger daughter, who finished college and became a schoolteacher in a distant state.

During hospitalizations the daughter was an overactive, assaultive patient who spent much time in packs and restraints. She was treated with intensive individual psychotherapy, electroshock treatment, and tranquilizer drugs. During her periods at home she usually isolated herself or became overactive in responding to delusional thinking. The family home was mortgaged to finance private treatment. Eventually the family finances were completely exhausted and she was transferred to a state institution. The father was able to get another business of his own started about this time. The daughter returned home after about six months in the state hospital. Family life at home was stormy with much family turmoil and psychotic acting-out by the patient.

It was at this point, six years after the onset of the psychosis, that the father, mother, and daughter began family psychotherapy. The mother inquired about individual psychotherapy for the daughter. Family psychotherapy was discussed in the initial interview. She was enthusiastic about the idea of family treatment. She was to discuss the idea with the father and daughter. There was no space for this family in the inpatient study. We agreed to do outpatient family therapy if the family wished to proceed with that plan, or we could refer them elsewhere for individual psychotherapy. Since there was no space on the inpatient ward, it would be necessary for them to again use the state hospital if the daughter required hospitalization. The father was noncommittal. The daughter said she needed freedom, not treatment. There was another family fight. The mother moved away from home saying that she would return only after the father and daughter had made the first appointment for family therapy. About ten days later the father called and asked for an appointment.

This series of events has been a common pattern with the research families. The parent in the adequate decision-making position is usually the one who asks about treatment. It is common for other family members to oppose either actively or passively. The decision-making parent usually asks the therapist to persuade the opposing members in favor of the psychotherapy effort. The therapists have been complete failures at this, but the adequate parent, the functioning leader of the family, has ways to overcome the resistance. We have made it a basic rule to respect the one in the adequate position as family leader and negotiator. For instance, the therapist may say that he wants one family member to be the spokesman and negotiator for arrangements, like making or changing appointments, but the family may designate another spokesman any time they wish. The families with the most active intrafamily resistance, emotion, and disagreement have done the best in psychotherapy.

Now to a summary of 84 hours of family psychotherapy that has now covered a period of 15 months. The mother decided to begin with 2 hours a week. Our first basic rule is that the family work on its own problem in the hour while the therapist observes from the sideline and attempts to understand and analyze the emotional process between the family members. The goal is to get the family to work together on the problem. When the family attempts to follow this therapy structure, intense anxiety develops. There are several ways in which the family attempts to avoid the anxiety. The most frequent is for the decision-making family member to engage the therapist in conversation. In addition to avoiding the family problem, it tends to encourage an individual relationship with the therapist, and the decision-making family member thus becomes more dependent on the therapist. Some families have been able to keep this going with the therapists for weeks but when the therapist is able to structure himself out of the "working-together effort" of the family, preferably by analyzing the family effort to avoid the structure, another series of anxiety-avoiding mechanisms is seen. The next most frequent is for the parents to talk to the psychotic one about the psychosis. There is the emotional divorce between the parents. It is extremely difficult for parents to discuss personal problems about themselves, but it is comparatively easy for either parent to talk directly to the patient, and this frequently changes rapidly to criticism of the patient. Other ways the parents avoid anxiety between themselves is by small talk or by silence.

The mother in this family opened the therapy with comments to the daughter about her psychotic behavior. The daughter responded with denial. This soon became a highly emotional denial and contradiction of the mother's statements. The mother said, "It is your unreasonableness and screaming that try my soul." The daughter said, "It is the things you do that make me scream." The mother continued to refer to the daughter as "sick" and to prove her statements with historical material. In response to the word *sick* the daughter's emotion and anxiety would increase. When her anger at the mother would increase to a certain level, she would suddenly shift to paranoid delusions and with greatly increased emotion scream that she would kill the boy friend who had wronged her. This boy friend had sided with the mother in one of the issues between the mother and daughter. The mother would yell, "Shut up, you will disturb other people." The daughter would cry. The mother would cry and say it was hopeless. The father would move to silence the daughter and say to the mother, "Don't cry. It is not so bad." Few things disturb the parents as much as hostile psychotic expressions from the patient. Family members are distressed by tears, especially tears in the overadequate mother.

The intense conflict between mother and daughter continued for about 20 hours at 2–3 hours a week. There were 2 consecutive hours that went about as follows: The mother began with a story that conveyed that she had been a good mother but that the daughter had been a terrible and ungrateful daughter. The daughter responded with stories to deny the mother's accusations, more stories to prove that she had been a good daughter, and more stories to prove the mother had been a poor mother. The mother would relate incidents to deny the accusation, more incidents to prove she had been a good mother, and still more incidents to support the thesis that the daughter was selfish and ungrateful. The daughter would then deny the accusation, offer proof that she was a good daughter, and more proof that the mother was a terrible mother. This cycle repeated itself over and over in these hours.

In our experience, a therapist can lose his way if he permits himself to become involved in evaluating the dramatic historical material that comes up in such hours. In these hours the therapist confined himself to pointing out the "proof that I am wonderful—proof that you are terrible" pattern. The vigor of the daughter's stand against the mother seemed a good prognostic sign. The inactivity of the father was most striking during this period. He was more a spectator than participant in the family problem. Both the mother and daughter tried to get him to take sides, but he successfully stayed on the periphery. The therapist then began to focus on the passivity of the father.

Clinical experience with passive fathers had a long background in the family-therapy effort. The one most striking pattern in the research families has been that of the aggressive mother and the passive peripheral father. In the first year or so of the project, we described this by saying, "The problem in the family is as much an act of omission by the father as it is an act of commission by the mother." There had been two families with dramatic changes similar to the family reported earlier in this paper. In these families the first to change had been the fathers, and there had been

striking changes in the entire family when the fathers became active, assertive participants in the family problem.
These changes would usually last for a few weeks and then
the family would revert to the former functioning. Two
fathers reverted to the inadequate functioning when they
developed minor physical illnesses. After the first change
had been possible, however, it became increasingly easy for
the fathers to pull up to more adequate functioning and less
threatening for the mothers to give up the overadequate
functioning. From these experiences, we would postulate
that a fairly normal family is one in which parents can
function in either the strong or the weak position, according
to the demands of the situation, without threatening either
one.

The project staff had been quite impressed with the
changes in the families when passive fathers began to participate in the family problem. We reasoned that if the first
change to be expected was activity from the passive father,
then the psychotherapy might be facilitated by focusing on
the passivity of the father. Eventually this was abandoned.
One family in particular helped to point up our therapy
problem. The therapist had been making comments about
the father's withdrawal and apologies. Gradually the father
became more active and assertive if the mother was at home.
She, as all the mothers have done, challenged his strength.
She asked him where he got his ideas. He said, "The doctor
told me I should do it this way." This was one of the incidents which caused the therapists to stick to analyzing what
went on in the families instead of trying to influence the
families in a particular direction.

This phase of the therapy with this outpatient family
occurred at the time that the therapists were focusing on the
passivity of fathers. The therapist said to the father, "You
never express opinions about family problems. It cannot be
that you do not have opinions." The father said softly, "Well,

I do think mother picks on her sometimes." The mother responded vigorously, "What was that? What was it you said?" The father said, "Well, I do think you start some of these fights." The mother said, "Name one! Just name one. Come on and get specific. Give me just *one* example." The father turned to the therapist and said, "See, I was squelched." The therapist said, "I just watched you get yourself squelched."

During the next hour the father was in a more inadequate position than he had been before. For the first time there was some mention that the father's new business might fail. During the next hours the daughter became increasingly psychotic, the mother increasingly strong, and the father increasingly peripheral and inadequate. The schizophrenic patients in our families have been like sponges for absorbing family anxiety. This daughter rushed in to bolster the anxious father, except that her help came out in psychotic schemes which she acted out in town. The parents began to hint at hospitalization for the daughter. She opposed them vigorously. This was a crucial period in family therapy. The parents wanted support for their view that the daughter should be hospitalized and the daughter wanted support for her view that she was functioning better all the time. To agree with the parents would be to support the family forces to "fix" the problem in the daughter. To agree with the daughter might delay the parents taking steps to protect the community from the daughter's paranoid annoyance of people in the town. The therapist tried to remain neutral. He made statements like the following: "It is the parents' responsibility to determine when you are no longer able to carry on at home. People go to mental hospitals when the family or when society asks for it. Many very upset people continue to live with their families. It is a family decision to determine when the family can no longer remain together at home. Mental hospitals do impose difficult situations for patients but the human organism is capable of growth when it has to adjust to difficult situations." The therapist said they should make their own decision if they did decide to hospitalize the daughter.

The mother made the decision and the arrangements to hospitalize the daughter. This occurred after 10 weeks and 26 hours of family therapy. There were many telephone calls preceding the hospitalization.

This brings in some of our other basic rules of family therapy. One is the rule about individual communications from family members who attempt to influence the therapist to an individual viewpoint through telephone calls, letters, and messages. The rule is that the therapist will discuss such individual communications at the next meeting of the family group. Frequently a family member will test this rule by communicating personal information by telephone. Another rule is that family psychotherapy can continue with only two family members present, but, if only one member can attend, the meetings will be discontinued until at least two can again be present. If only one member attended, it would be considered individual therapy. It has been our experience that when father, mother, and patient are present together and the therapist is able to maintain the therapy structure, the family soon encounters conflict and disagreement. This results in high anxiety, action, and progress in therapy. Any two members of the father-mother-patient threesome can successfully avoid anxiety issues and the therapy becomes more intellectual, more sterile, and less profitable. There was a marked calm between the parents the day the daughter was hospitalized. The mother reduced the appointments to once a week. The parents talked about visits to the hospital, the comments of the hospital doctors, and the status of the liquidation of the father's business.

The daughter remained in the hospital for three months. She spent half the time on a disturbed ward where she fought, defied the staff, and spent time in seclusion. She was especially antagonistic to doctors who called her "sick." She was psychotically angry with the mother for "forcing her into the hospital" and "controlling the doctors who kept her there." There were explosive scenes when the mother visited. The mother decided against visits "for the good of the daughter," but she encouraged the father to go regularly. After the acute upset had subsided, the mother visited again. The daughter agreed not to mention the paranoid delusions which upset the mother. She kept the promise but took up another equally sensitive issue which created a scene. She wrote one letter to the therapist in which she wondered how the therapist stood the parents and asking him to help her get out of the hospital. The therapist read the letter at the next hour with the parents saying that since this was family therapy, family matters would be discussed with those able to attend. If they wished, they could convey to the absent family member that he had received her letter and that she was probably more familiar than he with requirements for discharge from the hospital. Her acute upset subsided on tranquilizer drugs.

The daughter asked to return to the therapy hours. The parents arranged a hospital pass for her to attend one family meeting. She returned on the thirty-seventh hour after having missed ten hours. The following week she attended two hours. She was in a state of amazing intellectual insight but emotions were very controlled. Events shifted rapidly in the next two months. She remained home on a trial-visit status; the therapist went on a vacation; the mother went on vacation for three weeks; and she began to work. The absence of the therapist in family cases causes much less of a problem than in individual therapy. There was an anxious period before the mother left. The daughter presented a "I cannot get along without you" picture to the mother. The mother started to cancel a trip planned sometime before.

The therapist asked if the mother was treating the daughter as if she really were helpless. The day after the mother left, the daughter found a job as a file clerk. She worked, kept house for the father, and cooked. She was extremely anxious and concerned that she would be fired, but the father's unexcited do-nothing attitude seemed helpful. If the mother had been present she undoubtedly would have been on the telephone to fight the daughter's battles. Therapy hours were calm and uneventful during the absence of the mother. The therapist made comments like, "What will happen if she is fired? Will she collapse or disintegrate, or will she learn from the experience?" The girl lost her job the week the mother returned, but she immediately found another on her own initiative.

The therapy remained uneventful after the mother returned. There had been some changes. The daughter was working but still very anxious. The mother was more detached and less influenced by the daughter's anxiety. Instead of becoming overhelpful and advising, she could now say, "Make up your own mind what you want to do and do it." The daughter complained of lack of motivation. She said, "My spirit, my imagination, my fight is all gone. Unless I can get back my fight, I am sunk. It is the tranquilizers. It is awful not to be anxious in situations in which anyone would be anxious." She begged the doctors to stop the drug. The mother insisted that it be continued. The question of "sick" came up again.

This issue and the use of diagnostic labels is very important in these families. In all ten families there is a pattern in which the patient becomes the scapegoat of the family problem. It is inaccurate to say that the patient is a "victim" in this process. In our experience, the parents and patients all participate in this process by which the family problem locates in the patient. This has been a long-term shifting process in the family. On the day the shifting process is finally given a diagnostic label and is officially located in the person of the patient, a big change takes place in the family. The shifting process is then more fixed and crystallized in the patient. This was one of the factors that led to our concept of schizophrenia as a process that involves the entire family and especially to our effort to treat the family as a single unit. Generally we have avoided the use of diagnostic labels and have especially avoided agreeing with the family process to fix the problem in the patient. In my opinion, this would be one of the main advantages if we had a family diagnosis instead of individual diagnoses. This issue about "sick" came up again in this family. They asked the therapist for his opinion. He said it made no difference to him what label they used. If they wanted to use the term *schizophrenic* he would insist that the family be called *schizophrenic*. If the parents were called *normal* then he would insist the daughter also be called *normal*. The issue never came up again.

An impasse in therapy continued for about six weeks after the return of the mother. No one agreed or disagreed. Each would wait for the other to begin the hours. No one had a problem. They attempted to engage the therapist in social conversation. The therapist made several unsuccessful attempts to break up the impasse. The daughter was the one who was most alive and the one who introduced more issues into the hours. The therapist wondered if her functioning would improve if he devoted time to her problems. He decided to respond directly to her the next time she spoke directly to him. This was an individual relationship between the therapist and one family member. So, the next time she directed a comment to him, he responded as in individual psychotherapy. The daughter liked it. She came to life. The parents became interested spectators. At one point the mother started to say something. The father said, "Sh-h-h, let's see how he does it." Within the week the daughter telephoned the therapist twice. One message was, "Something inside me tells me to resign my office job and get a job as a waitress or dishwasher. Unless I do, I am afraid the 'real me' may get blocked. I know mother is against it. What can I do? Can you help me figure it out?" The therapist abandoned the trial at an individual relationship after one hour.

During the next hour of family therapy he made another effort. He said, "The family acts as if you are waiting on me, or time, or Fate for the answer to your problems. Somewhere I may have led you to believe I knew some answers. Actually, psychiatry has never found an answer to schizophrenia, though the premise of family therapy is that the family can find its own answers if they work on it." He said he was going to fall back and become a nonparticipating, note-taking observer. At the end of the hour the mother said, "Does this mean you will not see us again when you say we have to do it ourselves?" The therapist asked the others for their perception of his comments. The mother was amazed that she was the only one to hear the comments this way. This was the beginning of family discussions at home to find differences in the way each heard such comments.

The reason for the impasse in therapy became clearer. The mother had not resumed her adequate function as family leader since her vacation. The lead position had been dropped and the family sat and looked at the therapist. This helped to clarify our position on another basic rule: this is to support the family member who motivates the situation. When therapists have become critical of the family member who gets things done, they have found themselves with passive, complaining families that wait for the therapists to supply answers. This has been a greater problem with hospitalized families. It is very easy for the staff to become critical of the parents' actions and then for the parents to become inactive. Now, we would say to recognize the effort of the one who motivates the family, even if his actions appear traumatic or "schizophrenogenic." We have seen patients respond favorably to such activity from a parent.

In this family the mother was clearly the adequate one before her vacation. She was still the breadwinner. As soon as the therapist began to recognize her position, she moved immediately into the family lead and, after a two-months impasse, family therapy was under way again. She went into a vigorous attack on the inadequacy of the father. She said with great feeling, "I am tired supporting you. I wonder how I got myself into this position. You remain an unemployed executive while your family starves." This was the first real conflictual emotion between the parents. Previous conflict had involved mother and patient. The father made a plea for his inadequate position. He said, "This is the way you have always been. I am down and I need your help. All I get is your bitter tongue and your lashing out." The mother held her stand. She said, "You ask for my help! I have been supporting you for years. All I have done all my life is support you. Do you want me to support you the rest of our lives?" This phase continued for three weeks. The father made some changes. On a business trip he developed an acute intestinal upset and was hospitalized. An elective operation was advised. He returned home for the operation. He was hospitalized for two weeks and missed three appointments. It is not unusual for a parent in an inadequate position to develop a physical illness when he attempts to pull up to more adequate functioning.

The mother made her greatest progress during the absence of the father. This was 9 months and 60 hours after the start of therapy. She became intensely aware of how much her thoughts were devoted to the daughter. She wondered why this happened. She wondered why she always had the same feelings and emotions as the daughter. She recalled an incident when the daughter, then a child, had injured her head. Instantly, her own head had begun to hurt in the exact spot where the daughter's head was injured. She pondered the *why* of this. She concluded that her own life was connected with the daughter in some very complex way. She decided to "put an invisible wall between us so I can have my life and she can have hers." The daughter confirmed this fusion of feelings. She had never been able to know how she herself felt. She had depended on the mother to tell her how she felt. When she occasionally had some feeling different from what the mother said, she discounted it and felt the way her mother said she felt. She depended on her mother to tell her how she looked, if colors matched, and other such things. Away at school she could have some feelings of her own unless a teacher or some such person suggested she must feel a certain way. When she returned home she would again lose her ability to have her own feelings. The daughter then described her ability to know how her mother felt. The mother arrived at the conclusion that parents should let their children lead their own lives. Although she must have heard this hundreds of times, she reacted as if she had just discovered a fresh new truth for herself.

The mother activated this emotional disengagement from the daughter during the absence of the father. The daughter responded with pleas of helplessness to the mother. The mother said firmly, "It is your life. You decide." In the meanwhile the daughter had been very successful at work. She won the admiration of fellow employees for her ability to get along with a dominating woman boss. She resigned after three months to take a better job in the field of her college training. Her old employer offered to meet the new salary if she would remain. The office gave her a going-away party at which she cried.

The mother relinquished her lead position and there were two weeks of little activity in therapy. Then the daughter picked up the lead and began moving forward. She suddenly became popular socially. Her relationships with men were intense. She began dating several nights a week and staying out very late. She began going to parties in men's apartments. The question of sexuality came up. The mother said she would have to make her own decisions about this. The father was anxious. He objected on the grounds of late hours, the opinions of neighbors, and working with so little sleep. After about six weeks of this, the daughter called the therapist to ask for ten minutes alone with him at the end of the next hour. She said her problem was too personal to discuss with the parents. The therapist refused. He said this was family therapy and he would not change the rule. If she just had to talk personally, she would have to find someone else. The daughter talked about her problem early in the next hour. She said a boy friend was making demands for a sexual relationship. The mother said it was the daughter's own problem to work out. The father was very anxious but he spoke only of propriety. These comments seemed to be directed more for the parents' reactions than for their reality value. During the week, the daughter, without telling the parents, arranged a date to terminate the relationship with the boy friend. She returned home late. The mother went to bed early but the father remained up. This was another striking change in the parents. Before this, it had been the mother who was anxious about the daughter and the father who was calm and objective. Now the father was the one who worried about the daughter. He awakened the mother to tell her that the daughter was still out. She fussed at the father for disturbing her rest. When the daughter and her date returned, the father created a "behind-the-scenes" scene by talking loudly so the daughter and date could hear him. In the following therapy hour the daughter told the father that she was not pleased that he got mad but if he had to

get mad, at least he should have been man enough
directly to the boy instead of yelling like an angry ch

This series of events brought about a new equilibr
between father and daughter. The next hour, the seventy
seventh in 53 weeks, was another neutral hour. The daughter
had a new hairdo and was as charming, assured, and self-
contained as a young lady could be. The parents beamed
with parental pride and satisfaction. The talk of sex and
dates had disappeared. The daughter had met her old
friends from college days. She had been avoiding them
since her first psychotic break. She felt she would never
be acceptable to them again. She felt she could not risk the
pity they might feel for her. She had met one of the boys,
a successful young businessman who asked her to a party
with the "old gang." They knew about her long struggle
with psychosis but they accepted her as before, without pity
or anxiety. She said she had changed her ideas about people's attitudes to former mental patients. She said formerly
she had thought they were reacting to her but they were
really reacting to their own fears about mental illness. She
was meeting new people who asked how she had stayed
single so long.

The next 5 hours the mother shifted from her old adequate position to a weak, complaining, helpless position.
Each time one family member makes a significant change,
complementing changes in the others follow almost immediately. When the psychotic one improves, it is usually the
mother who becomes symptomatic. Before this time the
daughter would have become more helpless in response to
the mother's symptoms. This time the daughter held the
family lead. She said to the mother, "Don't try to dump your
troubles on me. I have my own life to bother about." The
mother said, "You can just move out on your own." The
daughter said, "Sometime I intend to marry and leave but

175

to speak
...ild.
...ium

e and not before." The next hour the
t the daughter go on in individual
daughter was now in a position to be
he father and daughter opposed this.
thought they had not exhausted the
therapy and he would not change to
the eighty-fourth hour the daughter
te position. The father had been employed for several weeks and he was moving toward a more adequate position in relation to the mother. This is the present status of a family that continues in family psychotherapy.

Summary

A clinical research project for the study and treatment of schizophrenic patients and their families was organized on a ward in a research center. Fathers, mothers, patients, and normal siblings have lived together on the ward as long as two and one half years. The theoretical hypothesis regarded the schizophrenic symptoms in the patient as a manifestation of an active process that involved the entire family. A psychotherapeutic approach, consistent with the working hypothesis, was developed. The family members attended all psychotherapy hours together. Four in-residence families and six outpatient families have participated in the research study and have been treated in family psychotherapy.

An attempt has been made to observe and to relate to the family unit rather than to the individual family member. From this viewpoint, certain relationship patterns became clear that had been obscured by the more familiar focus on the individual. Some of the broad patterns of relationship functioning, observed in these ten research families, have been described. There was an emotional distance between the parents which we called the *emotional divorce*. The family conflict seemed to remain pretty much in the father-mother-patient triad and to involve normal siblings less than was anticipated. The parents were separated from each other by the emotional divorce, but either one could have a close relationship with the patient if the other parent permitted it. The most common family configuration was one in which the overadequate mother was attached to the helpless patient and the father remained peripheral to the intense mother-patient twosome.

During the course of family psychotherapy there were some unexpected changes in the family patterns. A change in one family member would be followed by complementing changes in the other two members of the father-mother-patient triad. When the parent in the inadequate or weak position became more assertive and active in the family, the parent in the overadequate or strong position would shift to the inadequate position. This we have called the *over-adequate-inadequate reciprocity* between parents. In those families in which parents could resolve the emotional divorce, the psychotic patient began to change toward more mature functioning.

A course of family psychotherapy with an outpatient family was presented. This was a family with some of the most striking changes, though the change between the father and mother was less marked, and the change between mother and patient was more dramatic than changes in other families. It is our opinion that the theoretical view of the "family as a unit" can provide valuable theoretical additions to our usual individual concepts and that family psychotherapy may open up a whole new range of therapeutic possibilities.

References

1. STERNE, LAURENCE. *The Life and Opinions of Tristram Shandy.* Book V, Chapter VI, p. 372. New York: Modern Library, Inc.,
2. BOWEN, M., R. H. DYSINGER, W. M. BRODEY, and B. BASAMANIA. Study and treatment of five hospitalized families each with a psychotic member. Paper read at annual meeting of The American Orthopsychiatric Association, Chicago, March, 1957.

3. BOWEN, M. Family participation in schizophrenia. Paper read at annual meeting, American Psychiatric Association, Chicago, May, 1957.
4. BOWEN, M. A Family Concept of Schizophrenia. In *Studies in Schizophrenia* (Ed. D. D. Jackson). New York: Basic Books, Inc. In press.
5. ACKERMAN, N. Interlocking Pathology in Family Relationships. In *Changing Concepts of Psychoanalytic Medicine* (Eds. S. Rado, and G. Daniels). Pp. 135–150. New York: Grune & Stratton, Inc., 1956.
6. MITTELMAN, B. Reciprocal Neurotic Patterns in Family Relationships. In *Neurotic Interaction in Marriage* (Ed. V. W. Eisenstein). Pp. 81–100. New York: Basic Books, Inc., 1956.
7. SPIEGEL, J. P. The resolution of role conflict within the family. *Psychiatry 20:* 1–16 (1957).
8. LIDZ, T., A. CORNELISON, S. FLECK, and D. TERRY. The intrafamilial environment of the schizophrenic patient: the father. *Psychiatry 20:* 329–342 (1957).
9. LIDZ, T. Schizophrenia and the family. *Psychiatry 21:* 21–27 (1958).
10. JACKSON, D. D., and G. BATESON. Toward a theory of schizophrenia. *Behav. Sci., 1:* 251–264 (1956).
11. WYNNE, L., I. RYCKOFF, J. DAY, and S. H. HIRSCH. Pseudo-mutuality in schizophrenia. *Psychiatry 21:* 205–220 (1958).
12. BOWEN, M., R. H. DYSINGER, W. M. BRODEY, and B. BASAMANIA. The role of the father in families with a schizophrenic member. Paper read at the annual meeting of the American Psychiatric Association, San Francisco, May, 1958. To be published in *Amer. J. Psychiat.*

8

Somatotherapies in Schizophrenia—1958

LESTER H. MARGOLIS [1]

In the few short years since the advent of the newer pharmacotherapies, the somatotherapy of schizophrenia has been revolutionized. In order to appreciate fully just what has occurred and how this has taken place, it is necessary to review the status of the physiological approach to schizophrenia as of early 1953 just before the impact of reserpine and chlorpromazine was felt. At that time the techniques of treatment were few and their potential fairly predictable. Schizophrenia was treated principally with the drastic therapies—electroshock, insulin coma, and frontal lobotomy. There was a limited tendency to apply vitiated or modified forms of these drastic therapies to the more borderline forms of this disorder, but such efforts were largely futile.

Insulin-coma therapy was considered as the best treatment and proponents of this therapy felt that all schizophrenics should have the benefit of it as soon as possible after the onset of their illness. Even among those who attributed much of the benefits of this therapy to nonphysiological factors, its value in early cases was recognized. Remission could be expected in 75 per cent of those patients

[1] Assistant Clinical Professor, Department of Psychiatry, University of California School of Medicine, San Francisco.

treated within the first few months of the illness, and in 50 per cent of those treated during the first year, but in only an inconsequential number of those treated after more than two years of continuous illness. Because of the absence of controlled studies the long-term value of this therapy was difficult to document. The relapse rate was higher in cases with insulin-induced remissions, but follow-up statistics tended to support the advantages of this therapy early after the onset of schizophrenia or early in the course of a relapse. A skeptical analysis of "The Insulin Myth" by Bourne (1) drew little support and was considered for the most part as heresy.

Because it was simpler to administer, produced more dramatic results, and did not require the elaborate and specialized treatment setting necessary for insulin-coma therapy, electroconvulsive therapy was the most widely used somatotherapy for schizophrenia. Speedy remissions were effected in a high proportion of the very early cases. In those cases with a relapsing tendency and in those with affective features, the same favorable outlook obtained. In more chronic cases electroconvulsive therapy was less effective but still responsible for occasional remissions or lesser degrees of improvement. When utilized on a maintenance basis, it subdued the more florid aspects of the illness, slowed deterioration, and prevented relapses. In the more chronic schizophrenic reactions, its effect was largely one of controlling the aberrant, troublesome behavior without affecting the abnormal thought processes.

There remained the appalling fact that approximately one-third of all cases were total failures despite these treatments. These were the patients who eventually became candidates for a lobotomy. Quite a field of knowledge and controversy evolved about this procedure and approximately 5,000 such operations were being performed each year. The zenith of the psychosurgical approach took place just six short years ago in the summer of 1952 on the very eve of the era of modern psychopharmacotherapy when, in a period of twelve days, transorbital lobotomies were performed on 228 patients in the West Virginia hospital system (2). It is only fitting that this project should be under the aegis of Walter Freeman who had introduced psychosurgery into this country sixteen years previously and continued to be one of its leading proponents. Further insight into the status of this procedure and into the status of the other somatotherapies at this time is afforded when one reflects that the results of this 1952 West Virginia lobotomy project were so favorable and the other treatments in vogue held so little promise that an additional 285 West Virginia State Hospital patients were lobotomized in 1953 and another 115 in 1954. In evaluating the status of psychosurgery in 1953 Kolb (3) stated, "It seems to promise return to the community of a greater number of patients with chronic mental disease who have been hospitalized for more than two years than does any other therapeutic procedure."

In addition to these major somatotherapies there were a number of less drastic therapies based largely upon modifications of the existing therapies or designed to produce the same effect with a less vigorous technique. These ranged from carbon dioxide inhalation therapy, subcoma insulin treatment, and narcotherapy to histamine, acetylcholine, nitrous oxide, hyperthermia, and ether-drip therapy, nonconvulsive electrostimulation, focal electrical stimulation therapy, and photic-Metrazol stimulation, and frontal lobe procainization. Although each of these therapies gave promise in the hands of a few advocates, their combined effort succeeded little in reducing the ranks of the incapacitated schizophrenics. Nor was the influence of the then available drugs a decisive one. They were of considerable aid in the management of critical periods of behavior and in helping to render patients more available for therapy, but in well-entrenched psychoses they provided only a chemical restraint which was self-defeating because, while disturbed behavior was being quelled, confusion was being increased and responsivity lessened.

Such was the status of the somatotherapies on the eve of the era of modern neuroleptic therapy. Before describing what has happened since this time, I would like to reiterate a viewpoint expressed by leaders in the field of psychophar-macotherapy who decry the fact that appellations, such as *tranquilizer, ataractic*, etc., have become a part of everyday medical parlance. These terms are catchy and lend them-selves well to clichés. These new drugs have been termed *peace-of-mind pills* or *don't-give-a-damn pills*, thereby subtly suggesting not only that this is a desirable state, but that it is one sponsored by organized psychiatry. From here it is but a short step to these drugs being promoted on the one hand as panaceas for geopolitical tension or being denounced from the pulpit as no substitutes for prayer: a far cry, indeed, from the original concept of *neuroleptic* therapy as advanced by Delay and Deniker (3a).

When these investigators introduced the term *neuroleptic therapy*, they implied a specific and unique pharmacological action in which a decrease in initiative and psychokinetic activity is achieved, not by global inhibition of cerebral structures, as occurs with traditional sedatives, but by a selective subcortical action—an action peculiar to chlorpro-mazine and reserpine and their chemical relatives. It was not long, however, before the term *tranquilization* was ap-plied to this action, whereupon a host of other drugs with quite different properties came to be regarded as "tranquil-izers." These "tranquilizers by association" included mepro-bamate (Miltown, Equanil) and hydroxyzine (Atarax), and numerous other drugs with a barbituratelike action, cerebral stimulants such as benzhydrol (Cogentin) and methylpheni-date (Ritalin), and even anticholinergic agents, such as benactyzine (Suavitil). To promote greater clarity of thinking it would be well to substitute the term *neuroleptic* for *tranquilizer* and to abandon the latter term altogether. But, recognizing that this term is so well-entrenched as to be difficult if not impossible to discard, and that the epithets *tranquilizer* and *ataractic* will continue to be used, they should be reserved for drugs whose action is uniquely or principally upon subcortical motor centers, i.e., drugs such as the phenothiazine derivatives and *Rauwolfia* preparations. The other newer drugs with a more global inhibitory function should be labeled clearly as sedatives.

In making this distinction, one underscores the difference between the old and the new in psychopharmacology. The newer drugs with a primarily subcortical action lend themselves to a wide spectrum of psychiatric disorders but their principal accomplishment is in the field of schizophrenia, where with vigorous and intensive application their effect far exceeds that of all other forms of treatment. That is, they provide a means of intensive and effective pharmacologic treatment by which the principal manifestations of our most prevalent major psychiatric disorder may be modified, controlled, or abolished. A clear-cut distinction must be drawn between this type of action and the one achieved with those drugs which have become "tranquilizers by association." The latter are clinically quite useful, but their ability to influence schizophrenia is little different from that of the barbiturates and bromides. Whereas the truly *neuroleptic* drugs can, and often must, be applied intensively, drugs in the meprobamate-hydroxyzine "sedative" group do not lend themselves to intensive use in what might be called *corrective* therapy. Sedation and intoxication can be intensified but the clinical picture is essentially uninfluenced. Viewed in this light it is even more apparent that the only real departures from pre-mid-century psychopharmacology have been achieved with the chlorpromazine and reserpine family of compounds, the action of the other newer so-called tranquilizers being an improvement upon but not otherwise different from the traditional barbiturate-bromide sedative compounds.

This concept greatly simplifies our approach toward an understanding of the place of these drugs in psychiatry. Both the older and newer sedatives can be used as symptomatic and adjunctive treatment in the ordinary office practice of medicine and psychiatry, but they have only a small place in the treatment of major psychiatric disorders. While the neuroleptic compounds can be utilized in small doses as symptomatic treatment of lesser psychiatric disorders and although their side reactions and lack of euphoriant properties discourage the neurotic from overusing them, their function in such conditions is not remarkably different from that of the "lesser tranquilizers"—i.e., primarily symptomatic or sedative. Their unique value is in the treatment of psychoses, where they must be applied vigorously and where the lesser tranquilizers have no really significant effect.

In the five years since the introduction of reserpine (Serpasil) and chlorpromazine (Thorazine) in this country, far-reaching and revolutionary changes in the therapy of schizophrenia have taken place. In summary, these are as follows: Insulin-coma therapy, which was once considered the treatment of choice and capable of effecting remission in 50–75 per cent of schizophrenics treated in the first year of their illness, has been almost entirely supplanted. Certain types of schizophrenic reactions, especially those characterized mainly by catatonic stupor or by life-threatening depressive features, may fail miserably with neuroleptic therapy and respond brilliantly to electroconvulsive therapy. This is the exception rather than the rule, however, and electroconvulsive therapy is no longer considered the most effective and is no longer the most widely used somatotherapy for schizophrenia. Lobotomy, which was being performed in as many as 5,000

cases per year and which was held to be more capable than
any other therapy in returning to the community schizophrenics hospitalized for more than two years, has with few
exceptions become a thing of the past. There is an almost
universal consensus that, despite the fact that it is a more
dangerous drug, chlorpromazine is far superior to reserpine
in the treatment of schizophrenia; and the latter is gradually
being discarded. Chlorpromazine itself is in the process of
being ousted by several more potent and less toxic phenothiazine derivatives. There has been developed a host of
other chlorpromazine analogues which are perhaps safer or
more comfortable for use in symptomatic, sedative, or maintenance therapy, but which are either too weak or too toxic
for use in the intensive pharmacotherapy of schizophrenia.
The neuroleptics have provided a means of keeping the
schizophrenic out of the hospital in the first place, or of con-
fining the period of hospitalization to a few short weeks or
months while an adequate drug regime is being established.
With vigorous pharmacotherapy tailored to the patient's
needs, it becomes possible to maintain and treat him in the
very setting in which his problems were engendered. Con-
tributory factors can be tackled directly rather than *in vacuo*
and at a distance in an institutional setting. The schizophrenic's place in life does not close behind him and his in-
centive for recovery is not sapped by placing him in a
crowded treatment setting where his therapy cannot be
individualized to his needs.

There is, however, by no means universal agreement that
these changes have taken place. There remain some authori-
ties who do not regard the neuroleptic compounds as effective therapies and who cite the fact that despite the numerous articles written on these drugs, there are as yet no adequately controlled studies attesting to their value. A few
maintain that insulin-coma therapy is the treatment of choice
in early schizophrenia and continue to employ it in the

treatment of the more chronic, anergic, "comfortable" schizophrenic. Some continue to feel that electroconvulsive therapy provides a quicker, more complete, and stable remission
in the acute schizophrenic and better control in the chronic
case. In some quarters reserpine is still considered as equal
or superior to chlorpromazine. Many, perhaps a majority,
still are of the opinion that chlorpromazine is more efficacious
than its analogues. Many favor prolonged hospitalization
and treatment in an institutional rather than in a home
setting.

The reasons for this disparity of opinion are many, but
they can be reduced to one essential fact: namely, those who
favor the older therapies, who consider chlorpromazine no
better than reserpine, and who regard the newer phenothiazine analogues as less potent than chlorpromazine, simply
have not had the experience to judge otherwise. The hiatus
between leaders and followers in the field of psychopharmacotherapy is far from being closed. Without broad clinical
experience one is too easily deterred by the side effects encountered, too unskilled in dosage techniques and in the
management of side effects, too readily discouraged by the
patient's resistance toward taking the medications, too lacking in confidence in the efficacy of the therapy to pursue it
despite all obstacles, and too ready to abandon it in favor of
the simpler, more familiar traditional approach. The fact is
that, with carefully administered, vigorous, neuroleptic therapy, with skillful coadministration of ancillary medications
to control side effects, with dosage individualized to the
patient's needs, tolerance, and clinical response, the results
in all but a few cases are decidedly superior to the traditional
somatic therapies. It must be recognized that the institution
of a successful psychopharmacotherapeutic program requires
much more effort on the part of the therapist, consumes more
of his time, and is far more complex than one employing the
traditional therapies. Furthermore, neuroleptic therapy as-

sumes dimensions different from the older somatotherapies and cannot be compared directly with them.

In the past it has been standard practice to compare therapeutic methods by utilizing them on comparable groups of patients selected by random sampling, administering them in identical treatment settings over stated intervals of time and with similar follow-up periods. By studying comparable groups concurrently, or by the switch-over technique, or by treating patients who were failures with one type of treatment with another method, it was felt that a fairly reliable evaluation of the relative efficacy of the somatotherapies could be obtained. While such an approach is suitable for therapies designed for administration over circumscribed periods of time, it cannot be applied in matching such therapies with the psychopharmacotherapies. Only in those patients who achieve a full remission in short order can neuroleptic therapy be administered in terms of a "course" and be compared with a "course" or "series" of insulin-coma or electroconvulsive therapy. In all other patients, in all those who achieve lesser degrees of remission, or who remain relatively unimproved, the neuroleptic therapy should be continued far beyond the usual duration of insulin-coma or electroconvulsive therapy. In such cases the treatment may be said to begin where the other somatotherapies leave off. It should be continued in as vigorous a fashion as is necessary to banish the principal manifestations of the schizophrenic disorder, or, failing in this, in as intensive a manner as the patient's tolerance will permit, this tolerance meanwhile being bolstered by antiparkinson agents, stimulants, cholinergic compounds, and other ancillary medications, as indicated. Only after rather prolonged, vigorous administration should one attempt to reduce the maximal dosage or withdraw the drug in order to ascertain the patient's stability on a reduced maintenance dose or no drug at all. In chronic schizophrenics this testing point is considerably beyond the

duration of the usual course of insulin-coma or electroconvulsive therapy.

Acute and semiacute schizophrenics may not require
maintenance therapy, but in chronic cases, no matter how
good the adjustment under pharmacotherapy, the chances of
relapse upon withdrawal of the drug are great. In most cases
maintenance dosage may be relatively low, but in many
quite chronic cases maximal or submaximal dosage may be
required. In such cases the balance between relative well-
being and a barely marginal adjustment is so delicate as to
be upset merely upon reduction of dosage from the highest
level the patient can tolerate. Far too often patients who are
alert, spontaneous, responsive, and free of overt psychotic
manifestations while under heavy medication, become in-
attentive, absent-minded, preoccupied, tense, and manner-
istic when dosage is reduced. Psychotherapy which was
difficult at best becomes even more so. The dose required
to maintain this balance may be higher than most institutions and most therapists care to use, or one which they will
use for only short periods rather than for the prolonged administration so often necessary to extract the full potential of
the treatment. The importance of prolonged, vigorous, intensive treatment bordering on the patient's level of tolerance
may not be vital in the handling of acute or relapsing cases,
but in the treatment of patients who have been refractory
to all known methods of therapy, it cannot be overstressed.
At this writing, it constitutes the best, and perhaps the only
hope short of leukotomy of reversing the unremitting downhill course.

Far too often, in handling the patient who is placed on
neuroleptic therapy after failing to respond to the gamut of
other treatments, both physiological and psychological, there
is the temptation to settle for relatively minor degrees of
improvement by not pushing neuroleptic dosage to optimal
levels. This approach is based upon the misconception that

a borderline adjustment is all that can be hoped for and that more intensive therapy exposes the patient to more risks without materially adding to his chances for improvement. There is the tendency on the part of some therapists to employ homeopathic dosage over prolonged periods even in this type of patient, because of the feeling that, while more vigorous dosage might prove more effective, the improvement would not be "genuine," and would actually prevent their doing "therapy" with the patient. Another factor which might operate to favor a homeopathic dosage schedule is the possibility that more intensive therapy might quickly improve the patient to the point where he could leave the hospital and be cared for at home. At this writing many therapists are compelled by circumstances beyond their control to confine their practices to an institutional setting; many hospitals are too isolated geographically to permit patients to return for office visits; and other institutions have not yet succumbed to the inevitable demand for outpatient facilities. Until these factors are corrected the utilization of a more vigorous drug regime will serve to break the tie between patient and therapist and the fruits of this relationship will be lost to both parties. The fact that such factors may operate to dictate not only choice of therapy but the manner in which it is applied obligates the physician more than ever before to inspect his therapeutic approach to insure that the patient is not being fitted into a procrustean bed.

Because the newer drugs provide a really effective somatotherapy, which, in contradistinction to the older therapies, is suitable for prolonged administration, and, unlike electroconvulsive therapy, is not attended by confusion and amnesia, and which enables patients once destined for interminable hospitalization to be cared for at home, they add new dimensions to the treatment of schizophrenia. Paradoxically, while they provide the most effective somatotherapy for schizophrenia, they make it no longer possible to treat the patient by somatotherapy alone. With them the patient can and must be treated with full knowledge that he has problems and conflicts, in a clear setting which necessitates that an ongoing relationship be established with some one individual in whom the patient can have confidence and with whose help he can cope with the problems which contributed to his illness and which continue to plague him after he improves. With them there is the possibility of bringing the psychosis under control without hospitalization, or after only a few weeks or months of hospitalization, so that the major portion of the patient's care can be administered in a home setting. This will have the two-fold effect of challenging the family to meet the needs of the schizophrenic and at the same time militate against the deteriorating monotony and regimentation that, despite efforts to the contrary, so often become a part of prolonged hospitalization. It enables the family to take an active part in the patient's treatment and necessitates that it do so.

In these ways neuroleptic therapy assumes dimensions different from the older somatotherapies. It is different in time; it cannot be administered in finite "courses"; its important aspects often begin where the conventional therapies leave off. It is different in depth; it makes it no longer possible to treat schizophrenia by somatotherapy alone. It is different in scope; it makes it possible to conduct the major portion of the patient's treatment in the home setting; it increases the opportunity of the family to participate in treatment and may even force it to do so.

Earlier in this report the statement was made that chlorpromazine was being ousted by several more potent and less toxic phenothiazine derivatives and that a host of other phenothiazine analogues have been developed which are useful in symptomatic, sedative, or maintenance therapy but too weak or too toxic for use in the intensive pharmacotherapy of schizophrenia.

The initial modification of the chlorpromazine structure involved the removal of the chlorine radical in the hope that this would reduce the incidence of jaundice and agranulocytosis. This resulted in promazine (Sparine), a compound markedly weaker and with less therapeutic range than chlorpromazine, and with which jaundice and agranulocytosis, although reduced in frequency, continue to occur. There is, however, almost no "cross-over" in sensitivity so that patients developing jaundice with chlorpromazine stand a reasonable chance of not developing this complication with promazine. When utilized in large doses in intensive therapy, there is a 25 per cent incidence of convulsive seizures which is considerably higher than with chlorpromazine. In general, although this drug may be as suitable and somewhat more safe for office practice and is an effective emergency sedative, its therapeutic potency is considerably lower than that of chlorpromazine, and, in the treatment of schizophrenia, doses which border on the toxic are necessary to secure improvement comparable with that obtained with chlorpromazine.

Another attempt to reduce side effects while retaining potency involved the substitution of the piperidine ring in place of the simple amino group in chlorpromazine. One such compound, designated NP-207, rivaled chlorpromazine in effectiveness and seemed to show almost no undesirable side effects but had to be abandoned because it produced toxic retinitis. Many similar compounds have been tested and thioridazine (Mellaril), the most promising of these, is now being investigated clinically. It does not produce extrapyramidal dysfunction and in this way is different from most of the other phenothiazine derivatives under study. Because of the prevailing opinion that neuroleptic potency and influence upon the extrapyramidal system are inseparably linked, the proving out of this agent is awaited with interest. Lethargy and somnolence appear to be its principal side effects in heavy dosage. Mepazine (Pacatal), another drug with a similar structure but which is not halogenated, appears to be one of the weakest and most toxic of the phenothiazines. Jaundice and agranulocytosis have been encountered with it, and its autonomic effects are severe. Confusion and ataxia may occur with higher dosage, and it is not the drug of choice for intensive therapy. There are, nevertheless, many favorable reports concerning its use in lower dosage in office practice.

The truly effective phenothiazine derivatives are those with a piperazine ring in the side chain, those halogenated with fluorine, and those which combine both these features.

Triflupromazine (Vesprin), in which CF_3 is substituted for the chlorine radical in chlorpromazine, is approximately three times as potent as chlorpromazine on a mg-per-mg basis. It produces a higher incidence of extrapyramidal dysfunction, but its clinical effects are otherwise quite similar to those of chlorpromazine. It has been in use for approximately a year and gives promise of being capable of matching the therapeutic effects of chlorpromazine without as much accompanying sedation. No cases of jaundice have been cited, but only recently Ayd (4) reported a case of agranulocytosis.

Many times more potent than chlorpromazine, accompanied by less sedation, lethargy, and autonomic side effects, and thus far free of toxic effects upon the liver or bone marrow, the piperazine substituted phenothiazines appear destined to replace the parent drug in the treatment of schizophrenia. Chlorpromazine, because it is the oldest, most familiar, and "proved" drug, continues to be the most widely used neuroleptic, but it is only a matter of time before the superiority of the piperazine substituted phenothiazines is recognized. Two members of this group, perphenazine (Trilafon) and prochlorperazine (Compazine), have been in use for approximately two years, and those in the vanguard in the field of psychopharmacology are of the opinion that their superiority over chlorpromazine in the treatment of schizophrenia has been amply demonstrated. It remains to be seen whether these older compounds will lose favor to thiopropazate (Dartal) or trifluoperazine (Stelazine), both of which are in the investigative phase. The latter compound is the trifluorinated form of prochlorperazine and combines the potentiating features of halogenation and incorporation of the piperazine ring. This results in the most highly potent neuroleptic compound thus far achieved, being approximately 25 times as potent as chlorpromazine. The newest drug now under study is fluophenazine (Vespazine).

These newer agents, triflupromazine (Vesprin), prochlorperazine (Compazine), thiopropazate (Dartal), perphenazine (Trilafon), and trifluoperazine (Stelazine) are respectively, 3, 5, 7, 10, and 25 times as potent as chlorpromazine and produce a correspondingly higher incidence of extrapyramidal dysfunction. Inasmuch as this dysfunction is such a common manifestation with those drugs which are destined to replace chlorpromazine and is apt to take various forms which are distressing, dramatic, and bizarre, it is necessary that we familiarize ourselves with it and its management.

The commonest of these extrapyramidal reactions is full-blown parkinsonism with rigidity, bradykinesia, loss of associated movements, masking of facies, weakness, tremor, salivation, etc. The next most common is a dystonic syndrome which may be episodic or sustained. It is characterized by intense spasm and myoclonus which may be generalized but is especially marked in the neck, facial and jaw muscles, protrusion and torsion of the tongue, forced movements of the eyes, torsion of the neck, trunk, and extremities, opisthotonos, difficulty in breathing, talking and swallowing, and great apprehension. The third type of extrapyramidal reaction is one of motor restlessness resembling the akathisia syndrome seen in striopallidal diseases and described by Wilson (5) as follows: "Not a few subjects of the disorder complain paradoxically that they cannot sit still or do so only with an effort. They must get up, or move about, or shift the position of their limbs, inaction having become unbearable." Patients with this syndrome may rock in an agitated fashion, pace the floor, kick violently in a bicycling fashion once they get to bed. This reaction is accompanied by anxiety, irritability, and insomnia. The anxiety may come in waves and may occur without physical concomitants.

Although these extrapyramidal disturbances occur more frequently, are more intense and more bizarre with the newer phenothiazines, they may also occur in various combinations with vigorous reserpine or chlorpromazine therapy. They disappear quickly when dosage is lowered or an antiparkinson agent is introduced. They are easily reproduced upon omission of the antiparkinson drug or upon elevation of the neuroleptic dosage. By routine coadministration of antiparkinson compounds they may be prevented from occurring, and this in no way detracts from the therapeutic efficacy of the neuroleptic agent. They may be confused with anxiety reactions or hypomanic states or may simulate neurologic emergencies. Oftentimes their true nature as abortive or atypical extrapyramidal reactions becomes apparent only when they are seen to disappear upon the administration of antiparkinson compounds. There have been many attempts to explain these reactions on a psychological basis or to fit them into a psychodynamic frame of reference.

The parkinson syndrome is so stereotyped as to offer little opportunity for misinterpretation. Yet there have been efforts to "understand" this syndrome in terms of "somatic compliance." Freed (6) in describing an extrapyramidal reaction in a schizophrenic receiving triflupromazine theorized as follows: "He did not complain of the akinesia . . . only of a feeling of restlessness. It is undoubtedly significant that the patient paced the floors when he was disturbed by a problem in the past. Furthermore as a child he rebelled against his parents through 'bad behavior' in the form of overactivity."

Being more bizarre, the dystonic and akathisia syndromes lend themselves much more readily to misinterpretation. That these may be present as neurological emergencies is witnessed by the case of a physician who was hospitalized on an emergency basis 12 hours after taking a single 55-mg dose of prochlorperazine. His state greatly resembled tetanus and it was felt necessary to administer curare to control his spasms. Endotracheal intubation and artificial respiration through a "closed" system were then required.

Far more often these reactions are misinterpreted as conversion phenomena. One such reaction, occurring on the third day of combined reserpine and chlorpromazine therapy in a young woman who had been under analytic therapy for 5 years, was interpreted by her analyst, who by this time was thoroughly familiar with her psyche, as "a psychophysiological response to a deep-seated emotional problem." This "profound" disturbance disappeared when 4 mg of benzhydrol (Cogentin) were administered.

Azima (7) in describing patients who developed restlessness, insomnia, anxiety, and contraction of the jaw muscles while under triflupromazine treatment, pointed out: ". . . the aggravation was concomitant with the development of facial motor difficulties . . . and could be conceptualized as related to body-image changes symbolically perceived, by the patients, as threats to their potency (castration anxiety)."

There is little point in permitting such reactions to occur. Not only are they dangerous but they undermine the patient's confidence in the drug and in the doctor, and they can easily be prevented by avoiding too rapid increases in dosage and by routinely administering antiparkinson compounds at their onset. It is important to bear in mind that severe dystonic syndromes may occur with quite small dosage and that combinations of drugs tend to increase their frequency and severity. Of utmost importance is the necessity of recognizing these reactions for what they are, of correctly differentiating them from the anxiety and conversion reactions they resemble. Not infrequently, the development of motor restlessness and anxiety under drug therapy is mistakenly interpreted as evidence of a relapse and is handled by increasing the dosage of the very drug which is causing the symptoms. The anxiety is thereby intensified, whereupon the treatment, which might have proved successful in more experienced hands, is abandoned as a failure.

Summary

The years 1953–1958 have witnessed the decline and fall of the traditional somatotherapies for schizophrenia and the rise of psychopharmacotherapy. In evaluating the place of pharmacotherapy in schizophrenia, it must be stressed that the treatment of this disorder is an infinitely complex matter and cannot be solved by any one approach. The more successful the results of pharmacotherapy the more pressure there is upon family and society to meet the needs of the schizophrenic; the greater the demands upon medical and nursing time, the more need there is for psychotherapy, the more judicious one must be in the utilization of electroconvulsive therapy, and the more necessary it is to reorganize our thought concerning the manner in which the various nonsomatic approaches are applied. Although the formula "Drug treatment does good—as electroshock should," is an accurate appraisal of the current status of the somatotherapies in schizophrenia, it is far from a total answer to this problem.

References

1. Bourne, H. The insulin myth. *Lancet 2:* 964 (1953).
2. Freeman, Walter, Hiram W. Davis, Isaac C. East, H. Sinclair Tait, Simon O. Johnson, and Weaver B. Rogers. West Virginia lobotomy project. *J.A.M.A. 156:* 939 (1954).
3. Kolb, Lawrence C. Clinical evaluation of prefrontal lobotomy. *J.A.M.A. 152:* 1085 (1953).
3a. Delay, J., and P. Deniker. Chlorpromazine and neuroleptic treatments in psychiatry. *J. Clin. Exper. Psychopath. 17:* 19 (1956).
4. Ayd, Frank J., Jr. Fatal agranulocytosis due to triflupromazine hydrochloride. *Amer. J. Psychiat. 114:* 940 (1958).
5. Wilson, S. A. Kinnier. *Neurology,* vol. 1. Baltimore: The Williams & Wilkins Company, 1941.
6. Freed, Herbert. Some preliminary observations on the use of Vesprin in children and adults. *Monographs on Therapy 2:* 197 (1957).
7. Azima, H. The effects of Vesprin in mental syndromes (A preliminary report). *Monographs on Therapy 2:* 203 (1957).

9

Psychotherapy with Schizophrenics

Jurgen Ruesch[1]

Not only do schizophrenic patients occupy approximately one half (46 per cent) of the state hospital beds in the United States (34), but the number that live in the community goes into the millions. Generation after generation of psychiatrists have been challenged by the magnitude and intricacy of this problem, and the pioneer work of Kraepelin (28) on dementia praecox and Eugen Bleuler (7), Jung (25), and Sullivan (50) on schizophrenia is known to all. More recently Arieti (3), Bellak (5), and Manfred Bleuler (8) have reviewed the problems of schizophrenia in great detail; and those who attended the Second International Congress for Psychiatry, devoted to the subject of schizophrenia and held in Zurich in 1957, have received an impressive view of this world-wide problem (21).

A pertinent discussion of the social and psychological treatment methods does not necessarily include an answer to the obscure question of what constitutes schizophrenia. This subject is perhaps best treated historically (23, 55). More relevant are the developments of the last twenty years, par-

[1] Professor, Department of Psychiatry, University of California School of Medicine, and the Langley Porter Neuropsychiatric Institute, San Francisco.

ticularly in the United States where therapists have accumulated a body of knowledge concerning the treatment of schizophrenics (8) which is embodied in a number of excellent treatises on methodology (9, 10, 16, 19, 38). In spite of these pragmatic advances, we have not as yet developed a satisfactory theory of therapy with schizophrenics, although the beginnings are in the making (36). This paper, therefore, will not discuss methodology or over-all theory but will attempt to review the conditions, agents, and processes that today are considered therapeutically effective.

The Therapeutic Milieu

Social and psychological therapies with psychotics can best be carried out in a hospital where the milieu and the rules of interaction can be regulated and the participants selected (18, 24, 45). A therapeutic hospital community exerts a corrective emotional influence in the sense that it helps the patient to socialize more effectively. By focusing upon what goes on right then and there, the doctor and the staff concentrate on the patient's misinterpretations of reality, faulty logic, and misunderstandings of the communications of others (15). Such procedures, of course, are tested by the more verbal and active patients; and when they discover that no exclusion or condemnation occurs, even if they utter dangerous words or express secret thoughts, and that help may come not only from the doctor but from other patients and the personnel as well, they gradually become assimilated into the ward organization; and this process is in itself therapeutic (54).

In order to carry on open discussions in which delusional material and bizarre sensory experiences are shared, the patients, staff personnel, and doctors must be able to talk with one another. But if the participants come from entirely different backgrounds, they speak, as it were, different languages, and difficulties in communication may arise. Consequently, schizophrenic patients of the upper strata of society tend to be treated more frequently by psychotherapeutic methods, whereas patients of the lower strata tend to be given organic therapy (20, 37). It is not difficult to understand that the doctor, who by birth or education belongs to the upper strata of society, does not usually speak the lingo of the working class. He is not familiar with the traditions and the language of the lower class; and not being able to talk freely, he feels that pharmaceutical or physical methods might be more effective than continued futile attempts to reach the patient by means of verbal communication.

The psychological treatment methods, whether they are carried out on the ward or in the doctor's office, often arouse the suspicion of the patient. Many patients give histories of having been raised in families where multiple standards governed social relations. Such a patient does not believe that his interactions with the therapist and the staff can be governed by one consistent set of rules (40). In one patient's experience, the parents' communications were addressed not to him but to an alter ego or to an idealized image; and whenever the patient would deviate in his performance from the parents' expectations, he experienced rejection or condemnation (1, 2). In other cases, one set of rules may have applied to what was done and another to what was said; or one set of rules may have applied to the parents and another to the children. But once the schizophrenic discovers—and it may take him years to reach this point—that there are no hidden gimmicks, no secret rules, no unexpressed expectations, and that what is said is a truthful expression of people's feelings, he will begin to accept in part those conventions of communication and interaction that make such honest communication possible.

The Attitude of the Doctor

The psychotherapeutic treatment of schizophrenic patients requires a particular kind of attitude which seems to be characterized by acceptance of the patient's experience without condemnation of his sensory aberrations or reproach for distortions of reality. The doctor must be capable of empathy and must understand the patient's anxiety. He must have an eagerness to share and to establish a communal experience and a readiness to act if necessary (16). The schizophrenic usually tests whether the doctor underestimates the judgment of others, whether he can correct himself, and whether he is capable of evaluating his (the patient's) attitudes toward himself (51). It is important for the patient to discover that the therapist can stand tension and even abuse, that he can bear the fact that he is not omnipotent, and that he admits that there are many things he cannot understand (32). Above all, the therapist must be able to take behavior and action as a base line for reality and consider words, including his own, as secondary. No discrepancy between word and action should be manifest, lest the patient lose his confidence (41).

Recognizing that the schizophrenic's difficulties are with the nonverbal (39), certain therapists have introduced physical education, exercise, and activity into the program of rehabilitation. If the therapist, in a noncoercive environment, does things *with* the patient rather than *to* him, a notable improvement can be observed. Slow feeding, careful dressing and grooming of the patient, massage, manipulation of his limbs, active exercise, walks, games, and work programs play an important part, provided that the therapist participates and does not farm the patient out to another department (11). Most modern therapists agree that psychotherapeutic treatment of schizophrenic patients involves an active participation of the therapist, and much more so than heretofore has been customary (3, 13, 38). A confidential relationship in which highly personal problems are discussed and in which the physician is trying to work out practical solutions for the patient's worrisome situation is the most effective procedure. But in order to achieve such an optimal condition, consistent contact with a few people who care for the patient is of the essence (6, 53).

Withdrawal and the Danger of Sensory Deprivation

The notoriously low self-esteem of the schizophrenic patient is often concealed by social isolation. The patient avoids painful exposure of his low self-esteem by reducing interpersonal contact or by rigidly controlling the nature of the interaction (44). By reducing interpersonal exchange, the patient progressively narrows his feedback circuits until in extreme cases they may be confined to his own organism. The price is heavy. The patient experiences excessive feelings of loneliness, and when he shuts himself off from communicative exchange he cannot correct erroneous impressions (49). By depriving himself of the sensory stimulation inherent in human contact, he perhaps pays the heaviest penalty. Recent studies of sensory deprivation through experimental reduction of stimulation (30), natural loss of contact with the environment (35), or damage to the sensory pathways indicate that all three of these conditions result in an intense desire for sensory stimulation and bodily motion, increased suggestibility, impairment of organized thinking, oppression and depression, and, in extreme cases, hallucinations, delusions, and confusion (47). Clinically, we see the picture of sensory deprivation in persons who are temporarily or permanently blinded. Operations on the visual apparatus —particularly when the individual is older—tend to be accompanied by symptoms such as hallucinations or confusion (31). Apparently the schizophrenic's hallucinations and misinterpretations of sensory impressions are in part a result of the lack of external stimulation. In the event that such sensory deprivation occurs, the missing external input is replaced by an internal input drawn from memory or imagination; and this results in self-stimulation so that the total amount of sensation remains constant (33). Therefore, if stimulation should be a significant factor in the treatment of schizophrenics, one must bear in mind that to bombard the patient with talk, television, or similar impersonal stimuli does not suffice. Only when the needed stimulation is mediated through a significant person with whom he is familiar and whose behavior he can predict will the patient be able to benefit from it. This condition is very much like that of the infant. Proper food, diaper change, and clothes are necessary; but they do not substantially contribute to the infant's psychological growth unless one and the same person always cares for the child. Each time there is a change in mother, mother substitute, or nursing personnel, the child is slowed down or arrested in his development (48).

The Patient's Language System

In order to carry out psychotherapy we must use language. But the patient's tendency to withdraw results in disturbances of the language processes. The schizophrenic has difficulties with semantics. Instead of agreeing with other people as to what the objects or events are that certain words refer to, he makes up his own definitions. Instead of consulting a dictionary, he appeals to his fantasy. The schizophrenic uses symbols in an idiosyncratic way, and it is the task of the therapist to discover the private meanings that the patient attributes to the symbols he uses. The syntactic processes, which indicate the formal relation of word to word or sign to sign, are much less disturbed; and, strangely enough, schizophrenics do not show striking aberrations in grammar or calculus. The pragmatic processes, however, which include all the relationships between words and their users (40), are highly disturbed. The schizophrenic patient does not realize that signs and words are interpreted and that they are interpreted differently by everyone who uses them. The patient's poor mastery of discursive language is in part traceable to the fact that he has not learned the procedure of interpretation. In order to speak fluently and understandably, the speaker must abide by the conventions that have been established for the use of words; he must be able to distinguish a question from a command and an appeal from an informative statement. But unfortunately the schizophrenic perceives the words of others as instruments of control and coercion; and in his own use of verbal communication, he often plays with a word or a number as if it were a toy.

In verbal representation, an event is split into two components: a subject, which identifies—e.g., "the seagull"—and a predicate which qualifies and specifies—e.g., "flies fast." The subject-predicate dichotomy exists in all Western languages (12). The schizophrenic, however, does not share this orientation but prefers to concern himself more with the predicate. Instead of grouping his thoughts around nouns, he emphasizes that which is expressed by adjectives and verbs. This tendency is easy to understand if one remembers that the schizophrenic has remained arrested in his development at the nonverbal level. He experiences very much like an infant. He shows more affinity to sensations, such as "warm," "sharp," or "salty," or to perception of movements and action than to the notions that indicate what it is that feels warm or sharp, tastes salty, or moves. After all, color, shape, and movement can be perceived and experienced directly; but the identity of an object is something that has to be conceptualized and expressed in words—a process which can be learned only from others. And since the schizophrenic tends to withdraw, the predicate mode prevails in his experience and expression (40).

Bateson *et al.* (4) postulated that the schizophrenic's ability to discriminate between logical types is impaired. When a situation contains contradictory components, he is unable to react to either one and is caught between the devil and the deep blue sea. He therefore ceases to respond appropriately or to respond at all (52). Consequently the therapist who is successful in treating schizophrenic patients seems to be a person who avoids logical argument, definition, classification, and all those things that bear upon the subject of a sentence. If he can talk about fastness or slowness, about moving, or things that are green without ever specifying who, where, when, to whom, or for what reason, the patient understands him better. Once the schizophrenic has gained confidence that the therapist is a realist and not a victim of verbal unreality and that he accepts the perceptions and sensations of others, even if his own are of a different kind, he begins to make progress. Only after the patient has made sure that the therapist accepts experience in its totality will he begin to learn the conventions of communication. By then he has gained enough self-respect and sense of security not to fear further brainwashing by means of words.

Acknowledgment and Agreement

In a first encounter, the schizophrenic may fail to acknowledge the presence of the other person; or, if he does acknowledge him, he may neglect to react to the overt meaning of the other person's statement. Selectively and intuitively the patient tends to focus upon the ideas and feelings that the other person has repressed, emphasizing the covert meaning of the message (14, 40). These and similar observations led Federn to the development of what he called *direct analytic therapy* (13) and Rosen to the method of *direct analysis* (38) in which he bombards the patient with interpretations phrased in the language of the patient's unconscious. In this approach, the doctor works with what the patient brings with him and does not impose ways of communication which are foreign to him. Thus when the therapist feels in contact with the patient's unconscious—that is, when he understands the patient's nonverbal expressions and intuitively appreciates his emotions—the patient eventually begins to respond. It is as if the patient said, "There is no need to acknowledge a verbal fool; but if you are concerned with the things that matter to me, I shall respect you and acknowledge you."

This attitude becomes very apparent in an acute psychotic break. When a patient becomes psychotic, he relinquishes the verbal ways of communication that did not work in the first place; the ensuing regressive disorganization furnishes a random basis from which communication can be reorganized in a different way. At the time of the breakdown, the patient, with his primitive and uncoordinated movements, appears as if he were trying to relive the patterns of behavior that were frustrating in early childhood, in the hope that this time there might be present another person who would reply satisfactorily in nonverbal terms. If there is a therapist present who does not attempt to talk *at* the patient but who responds in terms of doing or touching, the patient usually calms down. It is as if such a patient knew that the basis for human relations is established in the nonverbal mode and that successful verbal communication cannot be achieved until feedback has been mastered in the nonverbal mode (42).

Unfortunately adult society looks askance at communication through action. Physical action of others is perceived not only through the distance receivers—vision and hearing—but through the proximity receivers such as touch, smell, taste, pain, and temperature, as well. Under ordinary circumstances, a person in our civilization has to deny himself or is denied by others the use of nonverbal modes of exchange. If he is, like the schizophrenic, particularly dependent upon nonverbal stimulation, he is liable to become frustrated; and at times the only solution left to him may be a psychosis. Strangely enough, if the patient becomes psychotic his nonverbal needs are acknowledged. All the successful behavioral therapies for schizophrenia are designed to further nonverbal expression, to stimulate the proximity receivers, and to establish feedback functions in the nonverbal mode. Among them are dancing, play therapy, psychodrama, occupational therapy, and such treatment methods as wet packs, continuous baths, and massage. Therefore, when an individual—be it doctor, nurse, relative, or friend—responds unequivocally to the intention of the patient and when the patient is given the opportunity to respond in return, the foundations have been laid upon which recovery can take place (41). Having been understood and acknowledged, the patient will begin to acknowledge in return.

But between the learning of acknowledgment and the ability to reach and stick to agreements lies an interval of years. Agreements can be reached only with the help of words, because the description of objects or persons involves abstraction and isolation of certain aspects. Buying or selling an automobile, for example, involves agreement concerning payment against delivery of the car; the religious and political beliefs of the participants, their marital status, and their culinary tastes are completely ignored. The schizophrenic, however, wants to test out the other individual in his entirety; he does not restrict himself to a limited transaction, and this of course creates trouble. The patient may learn, in continuous contact with the therapist, to isolate certain aspects of a situation. The doctor usually begins with the practical arrangements connected with therapy—time of appointment, the mode of payment, smoking, eating, sitting or lying down during the interviews. The patient must be made to understand that agreements are not coercive limitations that are imposed, but are voluntary contracts entered into for mutual benefit. By entering into agreements, the patient unconsciously accepts certain conventions of communication. That clinical improvement observed after a schizophrenic break is related to an increase in mutual understanding and agreement between patient and relatives has been shown experimentally (26). Whatever it is that happens in the hospital that leads to improvement thus seems to be based upon the patient's progressive acceptance of the conventions of communication. At this stage, the patient apparently is no longer threatened with a loss of identity or annihilation in the event that he should observe some conventions and enter into a limited agreement with others.

Coping with the Patient's Hostility

The infantile-narcissistic schizophrenic tends to overrate his hostility and consequently he considers this a blemish on his character and an unforgivable sin. Where the ordinary person represses impulses of violence, the schizophrenic is aware of them and condemns himself; and being afraid of what he might do, he imposes upon himself a state of complete paralysis. The patient combines self-censorship with fear of rejection; when he gets better, he asks for permission to be hostile and expects the therapist not to retaliate and not to reject. When hostility can be continuously expressed as, for example, in a hospital setting, few cataleptic states develop (17). But years may elapse before this state of trust is reached, and during this period the patient will prefer to withdraw on many occasions rather than to expose himself to rebuke. Most therapists agree that the hostility of the patient has to be coped with directly. Therefore the doctor avoids talking about hostile impulses either in commenting or in raising questions. Instead he indicates through gesture or context that he has noticed the patient's hostility, and he permits the patient to express and explain whatever he wishes. At times he may proceed with some rather dramatic interpretations which for all practical purposes reenact some traumatic situation (27). At this moment, the doctor uses the same blunt and concrete approach that the patient uses, always with complete sincerity and respect for the patient (19).

The Vicissitudes of the Doctor-Patient Relationship

Perhaps in no other disease does the personality of the therapist matter more than in the treatment of schizophrenics. Jackson (22) divides the psychiatrists who work with psychotics into the following groups:

1. Therapists with an intellectually competitive attitude who are engrossed in the productions of their patients and ignore to some extent what is happening between themselves and the patient.

2. Therapists who adhere to an interpretative method for handling the data obtained from the patient. They use "active" interpretations, and they tend to treat the patient as if he were more integrated than he really is.

3. Therapists who are cautious, talk little, are good listeners, and who are capable of establishing communication with the patient provided that he does not suffer from acute anxiety.

4. Therapists who are nonconformists, who overidentify with their patients, and are somewhat schizophrenic themselves. They are particularly successful in dealing with the acute phase of the psychosis.

These and many more types of therapists by necessity handle the problems of their patients in different ways. Therefore one must be careful in talking about methods of treatment lest one find oneself skating on the thin ice of verbal unreality. One treads on more solid ground if one matches the personality of the doctor with that of the patient and talks about a specific doctor-patient combination. Let us consider for a moment the problem of the patient's passivity.

His extremely passive orientation leads the schizophrenic patient to seek a symbiotic bond with another person who is omnipotent and omniscient and who at the same time expresses a desire to help him. This raises some difficult problems (29). A wish to devote oneself to another person (43) requires a nurturance that most people feel only toward their children. When a therapist displays such an attitude, it is in effect prima-facie evidence of either a personality disorder or a countertransference reaction (46). Nobody of sound mind exposes himself voluntarily to the emotionally charged and often destructive expressions and actions of the schizophrenic; but, fortunately for the schizophrenic patient, there are therapists who are not too healthy themselves. Therefore, both benefit and danger lie in the fact that the therapist may have some personal problems and in therapy may relive a situation which has been significant in his own life. This may lead to coercion of the patient and result in a behavior pattern which is not germane to his personality. Because he is extremely dependent, the patient's first impulse is to comply with the demands of the therapist. As a matter of fact, the anger that he experiences at being coerced may even be repressed for the sake of maintaining the symbiosis with the therapist. If the countertransference leads to such repression, it is extremely therapeutic: the patient has learned to repress rather than to withdraw. But once this stage has been mastered, the going may become tougher. The therapist himself may have an unconscious need to maintain the patient's dependency and his own omnipotent position. This represents the moment of crisis for the patient. If he terminates therapy, he will again be alone; if he continues, he may not develop any further.

The solution to such a dilemma is difficult, though not impossible. If the therapist recognizes that he prevents the patient's improvement, he can take on one or more new patients and most of his nurturant needs will be filled. The old patient then should be moved, either to a group or into the hands of a different therapist. The new therapist should be a figure who is less like a parent and more like a benevolent uncle. If the therapist does not pay attention to his countertransference, he may discover that the patient has taken things into his own hands. The majority of schizophrenics sense the danger of the countertransference, and after having profited from it in the earlier stages, they may begin to act out this conflict in the later stages. Sometimes the patient's symbiotic needs can be filled in a relationship outside of therapy, and in this case the therapist becomes the benevolent uncle; or the therapist may see fit to interrupt therapy for a year, after which time both patient and doctor have entered into new commitments and the roles have changed. Under these circumstances, continuation of therapy with the same therapist is feasible.

Summary

Psychotherapy with schizophrenics is oriented toward several goals: to cope with the acute anxiety of the patient, to alleviate his excessive feelings of loneliness, to raise his low self-respect, and to counteract his tendency to withdraw from social contact.

To influence the powerful inner world of the schizophrenic, the therapist studies those interpersonal problems that block the patient's development. Foremost among these are the inappropriate stimulus-response or feedback patterns that were established early in the life of the patient. Inadequate experience in the nonverbal mode prevents the patient from satisfactorily using his proximity receivers or engaging in physical or social action with another person.

Therefore, psychotherapy with a schizophrenic requires intense contact with one person so that the patient can learn to experience sensation and action in a flexible give-and-take situation.

To experience the self in a nonthreatening and communicatively rewarding social context may take the schizophrenic many years; and for the doctor, psychotherapy with schizophrenics may resemble very much the raising of a child from infancy to adolescence.

Psychotic periods with more intense disorganization and withdrawal are reversible phenomena which usually follow some threatening experience. These often occur during psychotherapy with the patient and may last from a few hours to several months. An intuitive understanding of the patient's conflicts and communication with the patient in the nonverbal mode usually enable the therapist to weather these temporary difficulties and to resume his long-term therapeutic work.

References

1. ABRAHAMS, J., and E. VARON. *Maternal Dependency and Schizophrenia: Mothers and Daughters in a Therapeutic Group.* New York: International Universities Press, Inc., 1953.

2. ALANEN, Y. O. The mothers of schizophrenic patients. Translated by J. Railo. *Acta psychiat. et neurol. Scandinav., Suppl. 124,* v. 33. Copenhagen: Ejnar Munksgaard, 1958.

3. ARIETI, S. *Interpretation of Schizophrenia.* New York: Robert Brunner, 1955.

4. BATESON, G., D. D. JACKSON, J. HALEY, and J. WEAKLAND. Toward a theory of schizophrenia. *Behav. Sci. 1:* 251–264 (1956).

5. BELLAK, L. *Dementia Praecox.* New York: Grune & Stratton, Inc., 1948.

6. BETZ, B. J., and J. C. WHITEHORN. The relationship of the therapist to the outcome of therapy in schizophrenia. In *Research Techniques in Schizophrenia,* pp. 89–95. Psychiatric Research Reports #5. Washington: American Psychiatric Association, 1956.

7. BLEULER, E. *Dementia Praecox, or the Group of Schizophrenias (1911).* Translated by J. Zinkin. New York: International Universities Press, Inc., 1950.

8. BLEULER, M. Research and changes in concepts in the study of schizophrenia, 1941–1950. *Bull. Isaac Ray Med. Libr. 3:* 1–132 (1955).

9. BRODY, E. B., and F. C. REDLICH (Editors). *Psychotherapy with Schizophrenics.* New York: International Universities Press, Inc., 1952.

10. BYCHOWSKI, G. *Psychotherapy of Psychosis.* New York: Grune & Stratton, Inc., 1952.

11. DAVIS, J. E. *Recovery from Schizophrenia: The Roland Method.* Springfield, Ill.: Charles C Thomas, Publisher, 1957.

12. DOMARUS, E. VON. The specific laws of logic in schizophrenia. In *Language and Thought in Schizophrenia* (J. S. Kasanin, editor) pp. 104–114. Berkeley: University of California Press, 1944.

13. FEDERN, P. *Ego Psychology and the Psychoses.* New York: Basic Books, Inc., 1952.

14. FENICHEL, O. *The Psychoanalytic Theory of Neurosis.* New York: W. W. Norton & Company, Inc., 1945.

15. FREEMAN, T., J. L. CAMERON, and A. McGHIE. *Chronic Schizophrenia.* London: Tavistock Publications Limited, 1958.

16. FROMM-REICHMANN, F. *Principles of Intensive Psychotherapy.* Chicago: University of Chicago Press, 1950.

17. FROMM-REICHMANN, F. Basic problems in the psychotherapy of schizophrenia. *Psychiatry 21:* 1–6 (1958).

18. GREENBLATT, M., R. H. YORK, and E. L. BROWN. *From Custodial to Therapeutic Patient Care in Mental Hospitals.* New York: Russell Sage Foundation, 1955.

19. HILL, L. B. *Psychotherapeutic Intervention in Schizophrenia.* Chicago: University of Chicago Press, 1955.

20. HOLLINGSHEAD, A. B., and F. C. REDLICH. *Social Class and Mental Illness.* New York: John Wiley & Sons, Inc., 1958.

21. International Congress for Psychiatry. *Transactions of the IInd International Congress for Psychiatry (Zurich, 1957).* In press.

22. JACKSON, D. D. The therapist's personality in the therapy of schizophrenics. *A.M.A. Arch. Neurol. Psychiat. 74:* 292–299 (1955).

23. JOHANSON, E. A study of schizophrenia in the male. Translated by R. Hasselgård and B. Walker. *Acta psychiat. et neurol. Scandinav., Suppl. 125,* v. 33. Copenhagen: Ejnar Munksgaard, 1958.

24. JONES, M. *The Therapeutic Community.* New York: Basic Books, Inc., 1953.

25. JUNG, C. G. *The Psychology of Dementia Praecox.* (2d ed.). New York: Nervous and Mental Disease Publishing Co., 1944.

26. KALIS, B. L., and L. F. BENNETT. The assessment of communication: The relation of clinical improvement to measured changes in communicative behavior. *J. consult. Psychol. 21:* 10–14 (1957).

27. KNIGHT, R. P. Management and psychotherapy of the borderline schizophrenic patient. *Bull. Menninger Clinic 17:* 139–150 (1953).

28. KRAEPELIN, E. *Dementia Praecox and Paraphrenia.* Edinburgh: E. & S. Livingstone, 1919.

29. LIDZ, R. W., and T. LIDZ. Therapeutic considerations arising from the intense symbiotic needs of schizophrenic patients. In *Psychotherapy*

with Schizophrenics (E. B. Brody and F. C. Redlich, editors). Pp. 168–178. New York: International Universities Press, Inc., 1952.

30. LILLY, J. C. Mental effects of reduction of ordinary levels of physical stimuli on intact, healthy persons. In *Research Techniques in Schizophrenia*. Pp. 1–9. Psychiatric Research Reports #5. Washington: American Psychiatric Association, 1956.

31. LINN, L., R. L. KAHN, R. COLES, J. COHEN, D. MARSHALL, and E. A. WEINSTEIN. Patterns of behavior disturbance following cataract extraction. *Amer. J. Psychiat. 110:* 281–289 (1953).

32. LITTLE, M. "R"–The analyst's total response to his patient's needs. *Int. J. Psychoanal. 38:* 240–254 (1957).

33. McCULLOCH, W. S., and W. PITTS. The statistical organization of nervous activity. *J. Amer. statist. Assn. 4:* 91–99 (1948).

34. National Institute of Mental Health, Biometrics Branch. *Patients in Mental Institutions, 1952. Part II: Public Hospitals for the Mentally Ill.* Washington: U.S. Public Health Service Publication No. 483.

35. NUTTALL, J. B. The problem of spatial disorientation. *J.A.M.A. 166:* 431–438 (1958).

36. REDLICH, F. C. The concept of schizophrenia and its implications for therapy. In *Psychotherapy with Schizophrenics* (E. B. Brody and F. C. Redlich, editors). Pp. 18–38. New York: International Universities Press, Inc., 1952.

37. RENNIE, T. A. C., L. SROLE, M. K. OPLER, and T. S. LANGNER. Urban life and mental health. *Amer. J. Psychiat. 113:* 831–837 (1957).

38. ROSEN, J. N. *Direct Analysis.* New York: Grune & Stratton, Inc., 1953.

39. RUESCH, J. Nonverbal language and therapy. *Psychiatry 18:* 323–330 (1955).

40. RUESCH, J. *Disturbed Communication.* New York: W. W. Norton & Company, Inc., 1957.

41. RUESCH, J. The schizophrenic patient's ways of communication. In *Transactions of the IInd International Congress for Psychiatry* (Zurich, 1957). In press.

42. RUESCH, J., and W. KEES. *Nonverbal Communication.* Berkeley and Los Angeles: University of California Press, 1956.

43. SCHWING, G. *A Way to the Soul of the Mentally Ill.* New York: International Universities Press, Inc., 1954.

44. SECHEHAYE, M. *A New Psychotherapy for Schizophrenia.* New York: Grune & Stratton, Inc., 1956.

45. SLAVSON, S. R. *Analytic Group Psychotherapy with Children, Adolescents, and Adults.* New York: Columbia University Press, 1950.

46. Society of Medical Psychoanalysts. *Schizophrenia in Psychoanalytic Office Practice. 1956 Symposium.* (A. H. Rifkin, editor). New York: Grune & Stratton, Inc., 1957.

47. SOLOMON, P., P. H. LEIDERMAN, J. MENDELSON, and D. WEXLER. Sensory deprivation: A review. *Amer. J. Psychiat. 114:* 357–363 (1957).

48. SPITZ, R. A. Anaclitic depression: an inquiry into the genesis of psychotic conditions in early childhood. In *The Psychoanalytic Study of the Child.* Vol. 2, pp. 313–342. New York: International Universities Press, Inc., 1946.

49. SULLIVAN, H. S. Conceptions of modern psychiatry. *Psychiatry 3:* 1–117 (1940).

50. SULLIVAN, H. S. *The Interpersonal Theory of Psychiatry.* New York: W. W. Norton & Company, Inc., 1953.

51. SZUREK, S. A. Childhood schizophrenia; psychotic episodes and psychotic maldevelopment. *Amer. J. Orthopsychiat. 26:* 519–543 (1956).

52. WHITAKER, C. (ed.). *Psychotherapy of Chronic Schizophrenic Patients.* Boston: Little, Brown & Company, 1958.

53. WHITEHORN, J. C., and B. J. BETZ. A study of psychotherapeutic relationships between physicians and schizophrenic patients. *Amer. J. Psychiat. 111:* 321–331 (1954).

54. WILMER, H. A. *Social Psychiatry in Action.* Springfield, Ill.: Charles C Thomas, Publisher, 1958.

55. ZILBOORG, G. The conceptual vicissitudes of the idea of schizophrenia. In *Schizophrenia in Psychoanalytic Office Practice* (H. A. Rifkin, editor). Pp. 30–39. New York: Grune & Stratton, Inc., 1957.

Name Index

Subject Index

A

Acetylcholine, 68, 181

Acetylcholinesterase, 68

Acknowledgment, of and by schizophrenic patients, 206–8

ACTH, 74, 75, 76

Acute schizophrenia, 78–79, 186, 188

Adolescence, schizophrenia and, 10–11

Adrenaline (Epinephrine), 69, 71, 74
  abnormal diversion of, 68
  cellular respiration processes affected by, 22
  central-nervous-system function and, 66
  chemical structure, 67
  metabolism, 15, 75
    faulty, 70

Adrenochrom, 67

Adrenocortical function, relationship to schizophrenia, 74

Adrenoxine, 67

Affective disturbance, 11, 12

Age of individual, schizophrenia and, 10, 11, 12, 74, 118

Agranulocytosis, 191, 192

Agreements, schizophrenic patients and, 208–9

Ambivalence, 11, 12

Ambulatory cases, 12

Amine metabolism, 80

Amino acids, 69

Amputation, study of, 90–91

Anatomical research, 16

Animal studies, 21–29, 33–56, 73

Anthropology, 99, 125, 141

Antiparkinson compounds, 194, 196

Anxiety, 63, 87, 151–52, 169, 194, 195, 196, 212

Approaches, present, to schizophrenia, 15–16
  biochemical, 61–82
  biological, 16
  linguistic-kinesic, 99–122
  neurophysiological, 19–57
  optimism in, 14–15
  physiological, 179
  psychosomatic, 87–96

Ascending reticular system, functional role of the, 31, 55

Ascorbic acid, 70, 71

Atarax, 182

Attitude, of doctor toward patient, 202–3

Atypical (borderline) cases, 4, 12, 13

B

Behavior
  linguistic-kinesic analysis of, 99–122
  psychopathic, 12

Benactyzine (Suavitil), 183

Benzhydrol (Cogentin), 182, 195

Biochemical aspects, of schizophrenia, 16, 61–82, 87

Body concept, 89, 92

Body image, 87–96
  defined, 89
  development of the, 91–93
  disturbance in schizophrenia, 94–96
  tests, 93–94

Body percept, 89, 91

Body schema, 89

Borderline cases; see Atypical cases